THE AMERICAN TORY

OLiGARCHY = A form of govt.
in which the power is vested in a few,
OR A STATE SO GOVERNED; ALSO THOSE
WHO FORM The ruling few.

THE
AMERICAN TORY

BY

WILLIAM H. NELSON

Northeastern University Press

BOSTON

First published by Oxford University Press in 1961.
Reprinted in 1992 by Northeastern University Press.
Preface to the 1992 Edition © 1992 by William H. Nelson

Library of Congress Cataloging-in-Publication Data

Nelson, William H., 1923–
The American Tory / by William H. Nelson.
p.   cm.
Originally published: Oxford England : Clarendon Press, 1961.
Includes index.
ISBN 1-55553-148-2 (acid-free)
1. American loyalists.   I. Title.
E277.N48   1992   92-31016
973.3'14—dc20

Printed and bound by Edwards Brothers, Inc.,
Ann Arbor, Michigan.
The paper is Glatfelter Offset, an acid-free sheet

MANUFACTURED IN THE UNITED STATES OF AMERICA
97   96   95   94   93   92   5   4   3   2   1

PREFACE TO THE 1992 EDITION

In the thirty years since this book was first published, there has been a marked rise of interest in the American Loyalists. As late as 1960 the two most useful general accounts of Loyalist activities and ideas respectively, Claude H. Van Tyne's *Loyalists in the American Revolution* and Moses Coit Tyler's *Literary History of the American Revolution*, both dated from the turn of the century. And for Loyalist biography, Lorenzo Sabine's *Biographical Sketches of Loyalists of the American Revolution* was still essential though it had been published in 1864. There were, it is true, several old biographies and collections of Loyalist writings as well as a few studies of Loyalists in individual states. One important book had recently been published, Esther Clark Wright's *Loyalists of New Brunswick* (1955), but it stood alone in the sophistication of its analysis of Loyalist attitudes and origins. Of journal literature there were only a handful of articles of any significance.

Since 1960 there have been more than fifty books and well over a hundred journal articles of importance dealing directly with the Loyalists. A good bibliographical essay on this work up until 1989 may be found at the end of Robert M. Calhoon's own thoughtful collection of pieces, *The Loyalist Perception and Other Essays* (1989). There have been six or eight general studies of the Loyalists and an equal number of books and perhaps a dozen articles on Loyalist ideology. There are twenty or so recent biographies, including studies of such leading figures as Thomas Hutchinson, Joseph Galloway, William Smith of New York, and Jonathan Boucher. There have been a few books and a number of journal articles on Loyalist military activities, a dozen or more major books and articles on Loyalists in Canada, and a group of studies of Florida Loyalists. There have been perhaps fifty articles on specific local conflicts between Loyalists and their enemies, many of these focusing on areas where Loyalists were especially strong. There have been studies of Loyalist women and of Loyalist communities, religious, ethnic, and geographical. There have been studies of Loyalist motivation, temperament, and psychology, and analyses of Loyalists by class and occupation. In addition to work pertaining directly to the Loyalists, much that has been written more generally about the Revolution and about the structure of colonial society helps explain them.

Broadly speaking, all the writings on the Loyalists address one or more of the old questions about them: Who were they? Why did they oppose the Revolution? What were their views? What did they do? What happened to them? As to who they were, my suggestion that most of them belonged to cultural, ethnic, religious, geographical or class minorities and felt threatened by a potential American national consensus seems to have held up. In particular, much of the journal literature dealing with local conflict appears to support this approach. The elusive corollary to the question of who the Loyalists were is how many of them there were. This remains unclear, and a determination of Loyalist numbers is a hazardous enterprise. A fairly close estimate of the number of active Loyalists in a given place at a given time can sometimes be made, but this takes no account of passive Loyalists, "neutrals," passive supporters of the Revolution, or sentiments that shifted back and forth with the changing fortunes of war.

The problem of Loyalist motivation has received a good deal of attention, some of it provocative but much of it unconvincing. In the view of some scholars, the Loyalists tended to crave order, hierarchy, and external support and to fear dissonance and disharmony. Others have seen them as individualists and nonconformists. Still others see them as timidly conformist and corporatist, and yet others as marginal and antisocial. Undoubtedly some Loyalists were all of these, though not all at once. So, of course, were many revolutionists. To attempt to apply current theories of, say, personality determinants to these vanished folk presents difficulties. In an individual case where there is sufficient evidence to form a clear picture of the subject's personal history and outlook, psychological generalization may occasionally be tempting. Perhaps Governor William Franklin's relations with his famous father, Benjamin, do partially explain his loyalism. The weakness of this approach, however, is that, at best, it can only be suggestive and then only in the case of a few of the Loyalist elite. Most Loyalists, like most of the people on the other side, did not make abstract individual choices of allegiance at all. They acted in response to a range of pressures, fears, interests, and prejudices—familial, local, economic, cultural. They deferred to those to whom they were used to deferring, and disregarded those whom they usually disregarded. They acted, not as "I," but as "we."

A good deal has been published in the last quarter-century on the political ideas of the Loyalists, some of it in books on individual Loyalists, such as John E. Ferling's study of Joseph Galloway (1977) and Bernard Bailyn's of Thomas Hutchinson (1974). Janice Potter's *The Liberty We Seek: Loyalist Ideology in Colonial New York and Massachusetts* (1983) offers the most comprehensive attempt to define a distinctive set of Loyalist political views. It is perhaps less easy to go astray here than in discussing motivation; even so, the ground is less firm than it may seem to be and there are false trails. To attempt to enclose the ideas of the Loyalists (or, indeed, of the revolutionists) within so doctrinal a word as "ideology" is itself dangerous. With a few exceptions, the supporters and opponents of the Revolution shared a common body of political thought. For a while in their deepening argument they emphasized different precepts drawn from their common stock of political ideas—the revolutionists affirming the supremacy of natural law over the British constitution as well as the right of revolution, the Loyalists affirming the legitimacy of British rule and the threat of anarchy implicit in revolution. From 1776 on, however, the Loyalists more and more often invoked arguments used earlier by the revolutionists, but directed now against what seemed the tyranny of the new republican governments. And, of course, within a decade or so, the Federalists were to defend established order against the threat of anarchy with many of the arguments the Loyalists had originally used against them.

Common sense strongly suggests (even if *Common Sense* did not) that much of the debate of the Revolution was simply that—debate. Arguments were supported, illustrated, decorated with examples and opinions drawn by both sides from many of the same sources. Both sides cited the same classical writers along with Grotius, Pufendorf, Montesquieu, Voltaire, Rousseau, Coke, Bacon, later Blackstone, and, above all, Locke. Only on the fringes of debate did authorities tend to be mutually exclusive—a few Anglican Tories preached nonresistance; Jonathan Boucher discovered merit in Filmer; and Tories made little use of the writings of the libertarian country Whigs who, Bernard Bailyn tells us, carried the radical republican thought of Milton, Sidney, and Harrington into the minds of the revolutionists. Differences in the political ideas of the Loyalists and their opponents there certainly were, as, indeed, there were within both camps. And political ideas were important in giving legitimacy and clarity to whatever stand people took as well as in providing a sense of rational rectitude. But political ideas were finally, as they usually are, more shaped than shaping—shaped, that is, by the fears and perceived interests that underlay them. One need not wholly share L. B. Namier's scepticism to grant the force of his observation on this matter (recently quoted in a *William and Mary Quarterly* Forum discussion by Gordon Wood): "What matters most is the underlying emotions, the music, to which ideas are a mere libretto, often of a very inferior quality."

One source of confusion in respect to the ideas of the Loyalists is simply the use of the term "Tory" to describe them. I suppose I inadvertently contributed to this confusion by preferring "Tory" to "Loyalist" in this book. I liked "Tory" better than "Loyalist" for these people because the latter term implied that their attachment to Britain was primary, while it seemed to me, and still does, that primacy should be given to their dissent from the views of their fellow Americans. "Tory" was, of course, for contemporaries a pejorative term, and the revolutionists applied it to their enemies to point to their disaffection. A few Loyalists accepted, ironically or belligerently, this term as applied to themselves. But except perhaps for a handful of Anglican clergymen the Loyalists were not Tories at all in the traditions of eighteenth-century English politics. They accepted, indeed celebrated, the Revolution of 1688; their defense of the British constitution and of parliamentary sovereignty rested solidly on Locke. Their most incisive and vehement objection to the Revolution was to the illiberal conformity it demanded. Most Tories were, in English terms, Whigs. "Tory," nevertheless, is a venerable American term for the opponents of the Revolution, and there seems no good reason to surrender it to the English who, after all, had taken it from the Irish and changed its meaning.

As to the last of the old questions about the Loyalists, what did they do in the war and what happened to them afterwards, these are easier to answer than questions of motivation and ideas considered in isolation. And here the work of the last generation has been especially productive.

Numerous studies of local political, cultural, and religious conflict, and of Loyalist strongholds, make it clear that the Revolution and the issue of American independence often merely intensified divisions in American society that went far back into colonial times and would, in some cases, survive well into the national era. Some of the work on the war itself, notably that of Paul H. Smith and John Shy, has brought a new subtlety into the study of relationships of partisans on both sides, not only to each other and to the British, but to a divided, uneasy, and frequently neutral civilian population. Studies of how the Tories fared at the end of the war and afterwards again show the range and complexity of the social relations underlying the immediate issues of the Revolution. There were places where Tories were driven out or even, occasionally, murdered; places where they were stripped of their property and rigorously prosecuted; places where leaders were singled out for prosecution or exile and ordinary Tories left alone; places where active Tories were deprived of *part* of their property by limited and almost considerate civil actions in the courts; places where Loyalists were allowed to return; places where they were invited to return; places where nothing happened to them at all.

Much has been written on the Loyalist refugees in what remained of British North America, in England, and elsewhere. Though perhaps less intensively than might be expected, Canadian historians have studied the later influence of the Loyalists on the political and social life of the provinces that were eventually to join in Canadian confederation. Still neglected, however, is the intriguing question of what happened to the Loyalists who did not leave. These, after all, numbered perhaps ninety percent or more of the total Loyalist population. A few journal articles deal with the later American careers of some of the better-known of these people, and the biographies of Tench Coxe by Jacob Cooke (1978) and of William Samuel

Johnson by Elizabeth McCaughey (1980) are useful. But apart from occasional flickers of light, most of the Tory rank-and-file seem to vanish into the republican society of post-Revolutionary America. Not all of them disappear quite without trace. In his book on Delaware Loyalists (1977) Harold B. Hancock described an election in Sussex County in *1787* in which the Tories drilled under arms, marched in military formation to the polling place, cursed and assaulted Whigs, and "huzzaed for the King" before voting. These Tory yeomen were, under the new Constitution of the United States, to carry on their old politics and old enmities, to petition for more paper money and for the removal inland of the county seat, and to vote Federalist in national elections. How many were there like them elsewhere in Tory backwaters where their local strength had protected them during the war and left them secure after it was over?

When I started work on the Loyalists more than forty years ago, the world of American history had just joined the rest of America in the numbing celebration of consensus that characterized American attitudes during the 1950s. Historians such as Charles Beard, John Franklin Jameson, and Carl Becker, who had tried to link the American Revolution to European revolutionary movements and European class struggle, were discredited and unfashionable. Consensus historians of the age, such as Daniel Boorstin, Clinton Rossiter, and Robert E. Brown, were confidently assuring their readers of the seamless continuity of American political life during the Revolution and after. Only a few beleaguered progressives, Merrill Jensen most notably, still insisted on the centrality of conflict in American experience. In this somewhat stultifying climate of agreement about eternal American agreement, what interested me about the Loyalists was simply their quarrel with their fellow Americans on the very nature of being American. Here, at least, was genuine conflict, even if it could not be fitted into conventional class generalization. What it should be fitted into is still a difficult question about Tory dissent.

If, not for all but for many of the people who found themselves in the Loyalist camp, the Revolution exposed rather than created their conflict with other Americans, then perhaps there are fault lines of American division that might be traced back to the earlier colonial period and forward, some distance at least, into republican America. There have been a number of recent attempts at synthesis in colonial history that recall, in some ways, the work of the imperial historians early in this century. Like the old, the new imperial history is hostile to American particularism and emphasizes the Atlantic and Anglo-American character of colonial America. But while C. M. Andrews, G. L. Beer, H. L. Osgood, and others saw colonial history in institutional terms and focused on governmental and administrative practices, the new imperial history is social, economic, and cultural and seeks to reveal the intricate network of processes by which the irresistible explosion of English energy across the Atlantic produced Anglo-American society. The work of Jack Greene and others on links among the commercial societies of the Chesapeake, the West Indies, and Britain comes to mind. So does Bernard Bailyn's work on British migration to the American colonies (*The Peopling of British North America*, 1986), and David W. Meinig's powerful geographical analysis of the English incursion into Atlantic America (*Atlantic America, 1492–1800*, 1986). Despite weaknesses in some of its generalizations, David H. Fischer's delineation of the cultural imperatives separating different English regions of American settlement from each other is suggestive (*Albion's Seed: Four British Folkways in American History*, 1989). If the lines of enquiry proposed in works such as these can be extended, broadened, and at the same time, refined, patterns of colonial society may become visible that will explain, more intelligibly than can be done now, some of the fractures evident in revolutionary America.

The text that follows is that of the original 1961 edition of *The American Tory*. The main argument of the book seems to me to have stood up fairly well. Judgments that I offered somewhat tentatively appear, more often than not, to have been supported by the work of the past generation. A few of my conclusions may even have anticipated some of this work. Nevertheless, were I to attempt now a general account of the Loyalists in the Revolution, I would go about it somewhat differently. But that would be to write a different book.

University of Toronto   W. H. NELSON

PREFACE TO THE 1961 EDITION

THE Loyalists in the American Revolution suffered a most abject kind of political failure, losing not only their argument, their war, and their place in American society, but even their proper place in history. As early as 1797, Jonathan Boucher, one of the few Loyalist historians of the Revolution, complained of the 'shameless partiality' towards the Revolution of the principal historians of the day, both English and American. Indeed, it was not until a full century after Boucher's lament that the Loyalists obtained their first sympathetic hearing from a major historian in the pages of M. C. Tyler's *Literary History of the American Revolution* (1897). Tyler's work and, later, that of C. H. Van Tyne helped rescue the Loyalists from ignominy without, however, explaining the depth of their quarrel with their fellow Americans, or the totality of their defeat. It is this that I have tried to examine and, in some part, account for.

Some explanation is necessary about my use of the terms 'Tory' and 'Loyalist'. After the beginning of open war in the spring of 1775, the people whom their opponents called Tories usually denied the name and called themselves Loyalists. During the years of mere argument before 1775, these people occasionally admitted to being Tories, but preferred to call themselves 'friends of government', or 'moderate men', or even 'the loyal party'. For the sake of convenience, however, and also because I believe the term relevant, I have used 'Tory' generally for the period preceding the War of Independence, and sometimes for the later period as well.

I began work on the Tories some years ago as a graduate student at Columbia University, and I am grateful for many kindnesses and much help to two men then at Columbia, Professor Robert Livingston Schuyler and the late Professor John Bartlet Brebner. My wife, Barbara Nelson, encouraged me to complete this work and edited my manuscript with a passion for logical consistency and grace of language from which I hope it benefited, but to which I am certain it cannot aspire.

W. H. N.

Rice University
December 1960

CONTENTS

CHAPTER I

The Roots of Loyalty

IT is not surprising that the role of the Tories in the American Revolution has been misunderstood persistently. The Tories themselves were confused about their essential position. Because they came eventually to regard their loyalty to Britain as their own primary political characteristic; because they called themselves Loyalists and forgot they had been Tories first, they have naturally perplexed historians. To see the Tories only as people who remained attached politically to Britain is, however, to distort their outlook and to ignore the necessities of their case. For many of them, adherence to Britain was, at the time, only an incident in their battle with other Americans over what kind of institutions America ought to have. For these people it was less a matter of staying with Britain, than of being left with Britain by the fortunes of war and the intensity of political rancour. Like all civil wars, the American Revolution was of slow growth. The Loyalists, like the revolutionists, were grouped together and were sent marching down a road of no return by a very gradual polarization of colonial society.

The mainland colonies in the middle of the eighteenth century formed an increasingly complex society, more fluid, perhaps more democratic, but certainly less homogeneous than in the seventeenth century. The decline of the French and Indian menace had removed a barrier to rapid westward expansion and had also removed the impulse to social cohesion that it had enforced on the old seaboard settlements. The advance of agricultural settlement into the Piedmont had produced an economic and political conflict between the new West and the older areas, a conflict sharpened perhaps by the contrast between the relative sophistication of the coastal towns and the provincialism of the back-country. Another unsettling influence was immigration from Ireland and the Continent which had made the Middle Colonies and parts of the South a patchwork of cultural minorities.

Along with new internal tensions and divisions, the colonies were beginning to feel new pressures towards a consolidation with each other. A greater mobility of capital and labour, a rapid growth of intercolonial trade, a common (even though rival) interest in the West, had made the traditional separatism of the colonies obsolete. That there was an increasing movement of ideas as well as of goods and population through the colonies, the social and intellectual ferment of the Great Awakening showed. Among certain classes there was a maturing sense of American nationality and interest.

The widening outlook of the colonists was not, however, exclusively American in focus. The new horizons of some Americans were European. This was especially true in and around the seaboard towns where two or three generations of successful commercial intimacy with Europe had produced a class of merchants and professional men with genteel aspirations and a cosmopolitan outlook. These people may have been increasingly estranged from the life of rural America, but they were less remote from England, in fact and feeling, than in earlier times. They found much to admire in the social and political system of eighteenth-century Britain. Like their cousins of London and Bristol, they respected wealth and those who had wealth. They believed in commercial probity, hard money, and the Bank of England. They envied the easy and efficient intimacy between wealth and government in England, and sought to reproduce it in America.

Years before the Revolution a number of men who were to be the Loyalist leaders were attempting to use British authority to establish and fortify local oligarchies in the colonies. It is true that these people usually thought of their political ideal as aristocratic, but it was necessarily oligarchic, given the absence in America and decay in England of a genuine aristocratic tradition. As Jonathan Boucher wrote, a little regretfully: 'In the present state of human affairs, . . . a man has, or has not, influence, only as he has, or has not, the power of conferring favours.'[1] The only patronage the American Tories could use was that of the Crown, and the Tory vanguard was made up of people whose attachment to, or dependence on, the British government was direct. These men included most of the royal office-holders: the governors, many of the provincial councillors and judges, the customs officials, Indian agents, and various lesser placemen. It also included the Anglican clergy in the Northern Colonies where the Church depended directly on British support. And the Tory leaders included a few politicians like Joseph Galloway and William Smith, men who were not office-holders, but whose fears or ambitions led them in an imperial rather than a national direction.

Here it is important to observe that what distinguished these men from other American leaders was not primarily their oligarchic outlook. For this they shared with most of the men who were to lead the Revolution and write the constitution. The notion that in a well-ordered society political power ought to be in the hands of a wise and wealthy minority was held by all kinds of good Whigs. What distinguished the Tory from the Whig oligarchs was that the former needed, and the latter did not need, support from Britain, since the Whig oligarchs could, and the Tories could not, gain sufficient support in America to hold power. The basic weakness of the Tories was not their attachment to Britain, for this was a consequence of their weakness; rather their weakness lay in the fact that they held social or political opinions which could prevail in America only with British assistance.

In the period between 1750 and 1770 there were several Tory projects requiring the help of the British government. The Anglican clergy in the North were working for the establishment of an American episcopate and for further government

[1] Jonathan Boucher, *A View of the Causes and Consequences of the American Revolution* (London, 1797), p. 218.

favours for their Church. In Pennsylvania the Anti-Proprietary party was trying to get Pennsylvania made a royal province in order to consolidate the power of the Philadelphia mercantile community. In all the colonies there were groups of ambitious politicians who had chosen office-holding under the Crown as the way to power or prestige. With the growing complexity of government in America there was a steady increase in the number of places available to such men. Some, like Thomas Hutchinson in Massachusetts and John Wentworth in New Hampshire, were on the way to becoming royal governors.

The expansion of the judiciary was creating a noticeable group of native American judges, like those who so impressed the youthful John Adams when, for the first time, he saw them sitting under more than full-length portraits of Charles II and James II, 'all arrayed in their new, fresh, rich robes of scarlet English broadcloth; in their large cambric bands, and immense judicial wigs'.[2] On a lower level there were hundreds of local officers of the Crown, gentlemen of substance like that estimable Judge Winslow in Plymouth, Massachusetts, who was the local customs collector, the registrar of the Court of Probate, the clerk of the Common Pleas and General Sessions of the Peace, as well as 'first magistrate in the County of Plymouth'.[3] For such men as these, loyalty to the Crown was more than mere, formal obligation; it was their security against the rough-and-tumble of colonial politics, against the envy of their less-favoured fellow Americans. It was more than a mere romantic gesture when in 1751, for example, Jared Ingersoll, the new king's attorney for the county of New Haven in Connecticut, began giving indictments in the name of 'His Majesty', and changed actions to run in the name of 'The King, Our Sovereign Lord.'[4] Such monarchical niceties as these were an essen-

---

[2] John Adams, *The Works of John Adams*, ed. C. F. Adams (10 vols., Boston, 1850–6), x. 245.
[3] *The Winslow Papers*, ed. W. O. Raymond (St. John, 1901), p. 144.
[4] L. H. Gipson, *Jared Ingersoll: A Study of American Loyalism in Relation to British Colonial Government* (New Haven, 1920), p. 40.

tial part of the Tory attempt to call the Old World into existence in order to redress the balance of the New.

The success of this attempt depended most of all on a continued willingness of Americans to tolerate British regulation. Therefore, the British government's decision at the end of the Seven Years War to reform colonial administration and to tax the colonies threw the American Tories into confusion. They were as indignant as other Americans at what seemed an unjust and arbitrary exercise of British authority. At the same time they were alarmed at the prospect of strife between Britain and the colonies.

For a time their indignation as Americans ran ahead of their alarm as Tories. A few, it is true, mildly defended the Stamp Act. Jared Ingersoll, then the Connecticut agent in London, wrote to William Livingston: 'I went to England last winter with the strongest prejudice against the Parliamentary Authority in this Case; & came home, I don't love to say convinced but, confoundedly begad & beswompt as we say in Connecticut.'[5] Most of the Tories, however, condemned the Stamp Act as wholeheartedly as did the Whigs. Indeed, Thomas Hutchinson, then lieutenant-governor of Massachusetts, made what was perhaps the most effective statement by any American of the case against the Stamp Tax in particular, and against parliamentary taxation of the colonies in general. Hutchinson's argument was contained in a letter he wrote to Richard Jackson, the undersecretary of state. He began by acknowledging the legal supremacy of Parliament, but he pointed out that, being Englishmen, the colonists ought not to be taxed by a legislature in which they were not represented. Like most American Whig writers, Hutchinson dismissed as specious the argument that the colonists had 'virtual' representation in Parliament, but, unlike James Otis or Benjamin Franklin, he did not think direct American representation in Parliament was practicable. He also dismissed abruptly the distinction between internal and external taxes which fascinated many Americans, and which

[5] Ibid., p. 137.

Chatham was about to take up. He saw correctly what the Townshend Duties were to prove, that the important question was simply whether or not Parliament ought to raise a revenue in America. He thought not, and he recommended that Parliament recognize that its power to tax the colonies had lapsed, either by disuse, or perhaps by the original removal of the colonists out of England. This was, of course, substantially what Parliament later did, and here Hutchinson sensed what was finally to be the distinction in England between 'legal' and 'constitutional'; what he really meant was that taxation of the colonies by Parliament was unconstitutional. In linking the idea that the colonies ought not to be governed by Parliament with a resolute conviction that they ought not to separate from Britain, Hutchinson came close to the principles along which the British dominions were one day to develop.

Hutchinson also pointed out that the colonies were already contributing heavily to British power and prosperity through their submission to the mercantilist regulations by which Britain encouraged her own trade. Of British expenditure for colonial defence, he made the same uncharitable assumption that Tom Paine was later to make, that Britain defended the colonies to protect her own interests. Hutchinson's advocacy of American rights went so far as to include an ironic apology for the violent tone of some American writings in opposition to the Stamp Act, which he ascribed to 'the intemperate zeal shall I say of Englishmen in support of what upon a sudden appears to them to be their rights'.[6]

There is, in fact, little to distinguish Hutchinson's view of the Stamp Act at this time from the views of such leading Whig opponents of parliamentary taxation as Otis, Dulany, or Dickinson. Like them, he conceded Parliament's *right* to legislate for the colonies; like them, he denied the equity of Parliament's taxing America. Indeed, Hutchinson went further in 1766 in opposing all parliamentary taxation than did Dulany or

[6] E. S. Morgan, 'Thomas Hutchinson and the Stamp Act', *New England Quarterly*, xxi. 461–7, 480–92.

Dickinson, but there was, of course, a difference in his methods: as a royal official, he conveyed his views to the government privately in a letter, rather than publicly in a pamphlet.

A number of other Tories were as forthright as Hutchinson in their opposition to parliamentary taxation of the colonies. St. John Crèvecœur, for example, pointed out that colonial purchases of English goods was a form of tax already paid to Britain. He reckoned that these imports, necessitated by the mercantilist system to which the colonies were subject, represented one-fifth of the product of American labour. 'These', he wrote, 'are the taxes that we pay.'[7]

Some Tories not only opposed British attempts to tax America, but defended overtly American opposition to the Stamp Act, and even to the Townshend Duties later. As late as 1768 Governor William Franklin of New Jersey vigorously defended the New Jersey Assembly in its opposition to Parliament.[8] And in 1769 that arch-Tory, the Reverend Jonathan Boucher, wrote in exasperation that the American cause was misunderstood and misrepresented in England: 'Seriously,' he wrote an English friend, 'I do think the American Opposi'n the most warrantable, generous, & manly, that History can produce.'[9]

It is clear that one obvious handicap the Tories were to suffer in attempting to uphold British authority was their own distaste for the measures being pursued by the British government, and their sympathy for what at first appeared to be an American rather than a revolutionary cause. This embarrassment undoubtedly accounts in part for the comparative scarcity of Tory arguments in the 1760's. Even as early as the time of the Stamp Act, however, a few suspicious Tories began, not

---

[7] Hector St. John Crèvecœur, *Sketches of Eighteenth Century America*, ed. H. L. Bourdin and others (New Haven, 1925), p. 94.

[8] W. Nelson and F. W. Ricord, eds., *Documents Relating to the Colonial, Revolutionary and Post-Revolutionary History of New Jersey*, 1st series (Newark, 1880), x. 64–95.

[9] 'The Letters of Jonathan Boucher', *Maryland Historical Magazine*, viii. 44–45.

to defend British taxation of America, but to question the ends and means of the more violent American critics of Parliament.

Joseph Galloway was, if not the first, easily the most alert and faithful of Britain's American watch-dogs. While still in his twenties, Galloway had become Benjamin Franklin's deputy in the Pennsylvania Assembly, and had been convinced by Franklin of the practicability of a closer relationship with Britain. The Anti-Proprietary party which Galloway led in the Assembly represented chiefly the conservative mercantile class of Philadelphia and the conservative farmers of the old counties around Philadelphia. These people lived in growing apprehension of the Scotch-Irish and New England settlers who were filling the western counties, and who seemed to the Philadelphians to be a violent and lawless breed. Under the decaying proprietary government, Pennsylvania appeared to Galloway and his friends to be drifting into a state of anarchy, a danger which the Paxton riots of 1763 had emphasized. Reform was imperative, but democratic reform seemed more threatening than none at all. The obvious solution to Galloway was some form of closer constitutional union with Britain which would give Philadelphia effective British support against the West. He had come to favour not only the transformation of Pennsylvania into a royal province, but also direct colonial representation in Parliament.[10]

Pennsylvania conservatives like Galloway had not sufficient ease of mind to join their brethren of Virginia in chanting the old Whig songs of liberty. The Stamp Act crisis threw them into confusion and alarm. Although few Pennsylvanians went so far as Benjamin Franklin in approving the stamp tax, the opposition to it was less exuberant than in most of the other colonies. In Philadelphia, when riots were threatened by the radicals, Galloway called out the *White Oaks* and *Hearts of Oak*, clubs of tradesmen, who posted themselves throughout the city and broke up the demonstrations of the Sons of

[10] O. C. Kuntzleman, *Joseph Galloway, Loyalist* (Philadelphia, 1941), pp. 24–25, 39–44.

Liberty.[11] Shortly after this Galloway wrote a long letter to the *Pennsylvania Journal* criticizing the 'impropriety and rashness' of the methods by which the Stamp Act was being opposed. He pointed out that Britain had run up a great debt in defending America from the French and Indian menace, while the Americans had been the chief beneficiaries of the peace settlement. He thought it reasonable to expect the colonies to contribute part of the cost of their own defence. As matters stood, this might be done by the voluntary action of the separate colonial legislatures, or by paying taxes levied by Parliament. The miserable failure of the former method during the Seven Years War had, Galloway thought, prompted the imperial government to attempt direct taxation of the colonies. He then suggested two other ways the colonies might share in the cost of imperial defence: they might ask for representation in Parliament, which, if granted, would give Parliament a right to tax America, and give America a voice in the management of the Empire; or, they might form an American union with a common legislature which could then, with Parliament's concurrence, provide for American defence. Otherwise, the 'law of necessity' would justify British taxation of the colonies.[12]

In a later letter Galloway deplored the riots against the Stamp Act, but he acknowledged the depth of colonial discontent, and he called on the British government, rather than on the colonies themselves, to propose alternatives to direct parliamentary taxation.[13] Galloway's enthusiasm for union with Britain seems not to have been shared wholeheartedly, even by his subordinates in the Anti-Proprietary party. He was to continue for twenty years, however, with more remarkable persistence than acumen, to regard the American Revolution as arising out of a simple constitutional problem, and to propose

---

[11] J. C. Miller, *Origins of the American Revolution* (Boston, 1943), p. 136.
[12] Letter signed 'Americanus', in *Pennsylvania Journal*, 29 Aug. 1765. Quoted in Kuntzleman, *Joseph Galloway*, pp. 64–66.
[13] Ibid., p. 66.

sensible solutions alternately to the imperial government and
to his fellow Americans.

Apart from Galloway's letters, the most important defence
of Britain to be made in the colonies in 1765 came, appro-
priately enough, from Newport, Rhode Island. As the apex of
the great trading triangles whose arms ran to Africa, Europe,
and the West Indies, Newport lived more in the Atlantic community than on the American continent. It was a little cosmopolitan enclave on the edge of Puritan New England. The town
was dominated by a group of merchants, described pleasantly
as consisting of 'about twenty genteel families, all intimate
with each other as if they had been the nearest and dearest
relations'.[14] The leader of the Newport oligarchs was Martin
Howard, an urbane and seasoned politician who had been a
delegate to the Albany Congress in 1754. In February 1765
Howard published a pamphlet in which he examined the
colonial quarrel with Parliament from a forthrightly Tory
point of view.

Howard observed that there was no accepted definition of
the constitutional relation between the colonies and England,
and that until this relation was defined, all reasoning, including his own, would be inconclusive. He thought, however, that
personal rights were being confused with political rights. The
colonists had all the personal rights of life, liberty, and estate
possessed by any other Englishmen, and these rights were
secured by the common law. But, he maintained, the political
rights of the colonists were limited by the terms of the colonial
charters. Howard accepted the sovereignty of Parliament: 'It is
of the essence of government, that there should be a supreme
head.' The 'rights of Englishmen' and the sovereignty of Parliament 'have both grown out of the same stock . . . and if we
avail ourselves of the one, we must submit to, and acknowledge
the other'.

[14] Robert Hunter, *Quebec to Carolina in 1785–1786: Being the Travel
Diary and Observations of Robert Hunter, Jr.*, ed. L. B. Wright and M. Tin-
ling (San Marino, 1943), p. 121.

[Handwritten left margin: MARTIN HOWARD Published Pamphlet from Tory Point of View]

[Handwritten bottom: ↳ Howard stated that there was no clear definition of the Relation between the colonies and G.B. when it came to constitutional rights He thought that personal rights were being confused with political rights.]

Howard doubted that the colonists really wanted representation in Parliament and, unlike Galloway or Benjamin Franklin, he thought there would be no great advantage in sending a handful of American members to Westminster. 'The right of representation', he wrote, 'is but a phantom.' Howard came much closer than most Americans to accepting the English concept of 'virtual representation'. He wrote that the freedom and happiness of every British subject depended not upon his precise share in elections, but upon the sense and virtue of Parliament, which depended in turn upon the sense and virtue of the whole nation. For his part, he wrote, he would rather trust the English who knew a great deal about liberty, than trust an assembly in Rhode Island where 'the law has scarcely yet dawned', and where legal rights were decided by transient and prejudiced majorities.

Concluding his constitutional argument, Howard insisted that once the jurisdiction of Parliament was admitted at all, it was 'transcendant and entire', and that in consequence Parliament might levy internal taxes in the colonies as well as regulate trade. The stamp duty was equitable, though regrettable. The colonists should petition and remonstrate against the Stamp Act, but much of the opposition to the Act, Howard wrote, would only 'embitter the minds of a simple, credulous, and hitherto loyal people, and . . . alienate their affections from *Great-Britain*, their best friend'.[15]

Howard's pamphlet excited great indignation in New England. The deputy-governor of Rhode Island took a copy to the Assembly and asked members to take measures against the printer; some favoured having the pamphlet publicly burned by the common hangman. Howard wrote a mild defence of his paper, in which he maintained ingenuously that his only purpose had been to remove prejudices and 'idols of the mind'. He expressed surprise at the bitterness with which his first pamphlet had been attacked: 'To apologize for Great-Britain, it

[15] [Martin Howard], *A Letter from a Gentleman at Halifax, to His Friend in Rhode-Island* (Newport, 1765).

seems, is the only unpardonable sin in this meridian.' Considering, he concluded, 'how thin the partition is, between excess of
liberty and absolute tyranny', he was grateful that 'in the last
resort his liberty and property were subject to the care of
Britain'.[16]

James Otis wrote a furious reply to Howard's second pamphlet, in which he fumed at the cosmopolitanism of Newport and
contrasted it with the purely English character of the rest of
New England. 'Such', he wrote of Newport, 'is the little, dirty,
drinking, drabbing, contaminated knot of thieves, beggars,
and transports . . . collected from the four winds of the earth,
and made up of Turks, Jews, and other infidels, with a few
renegado Christians and Catholics.'[17] Here can be glimpsed
the attitude that was later to damn as un-American any opposition to the opposition to Britain.

It must be observed that there was no Tory party in the
colonies during the first years of the dispute with Britain.
There was, to be sure, no Whig party either, but there does
seem to have been among the opponents of the British government a community of feeling and commonness of purpose
lacking among the Tories. Such occasional defenders of Britain
as Galloway and Howard are isolated and exceptional. There
was, however, one coherent group in the colonies that became
involved indirectly in a defence of British prerogatives at an
early date. This was the Church of England clergy in the
Northern Colonies whose own main interest in the 1760's was
the establishment of an Anglican episcopate in America, a
project which was the culmination of a long, slow process of
Anglican aggrandizement in the North.

Outside Virginia, Maryland, and South Carolina, the Church
of England in America had been very weak in the seventeenth
century. By 1700, however, some of the fire had died out of

---

[16] [Martin Howard], *A Defence of the Letter from a Gentleman at Halifax
. . . etc.* (Newport, 1765).
[17] Quoted in M. C. Tyler, *The Literary History of the American Revolution* (2 vols., New York, 1897), i. 78.

New England Puritanism, and in the Middle Colonies no one religious group had a privileged position. The Anglicans had taken advantage of their opportunity. In 1701 the Society for the Propagation of the Gospel in Foreign Parts had been chartered, and had very shortly become the agent of Anglicanism in the Northern Colonies. The Society's funds enabled dozens of Episcopal churches to weather early indifference and the hostility of the established dissenters, and the Church had made substantial progress, even in New England, against the Calvinist orthodoxy of the time. Many prosperous colonials of Puritan stock, as they gradually acquired liberal tastes, came to find the ordered conviviality of the Anglicans more congenial than the severe discipline of the Presbyterians and Congregationalists. While one effect of the eighteenth-century Enlightenment in America had been the appearance of free-thinking secularists, another was the growing number of Episcopalians.[18]

The Church of England's progress in the colonies, though fairly steady, was by no means smooth. The Anglican plans to secure an American bishop had alarmed the older Puritan churches as early as 1715. In the 1720's the defection to the Church of England of Timothy Cutler and a part of the Yale faculty had touched off a bitter pamphlet war with the Congregationalists. The Great Awakening had, in its turn, alarmed the Anglicans and, in the Middle Colonies, driven them into alliance with the conservative Presbyterians. The most notable fruit of this alliance was the College of Philadelphia, whose provost, the Reverend William Smith, was an Anglican, and whose vice-provost was an Old-Side Presbyterian.[19] Despite, or in some cases perhaps because of, the Great Awakening, Church of England membership was becoming, by the middle of the century, socially desirable in the Middle Colonies and fashionable even in Boston.

[18] L. J. Trinterud, *The Forming of an American Tradition* (Philadelphia, 1949), p. 229.
[19] Ibid., pp. 229–31.

The Calvinist clergy, particularly the New England Congregationalists, naturally resented the successful aggression of the Episcopalians. They worried about the unlimited resources their enemies could draw upon in England, and they were deathly afraid of an American episcopacy, a project the Anglicans renewed vigorously in 1766. While the Anglicans felt it an intolerable handicap that their ministers had to be ordained in London, the dissenters, especially in New England, were haunted by ancestral memories of 'that monster of wickedness', Archbishop Laud. They were afraid that if they permitted the importation of Church of England bishops, they might shortly have to support an Anglican establishment. These fears were given some support by the success of the Episcopalians in getting their Church partially established in the counties around New York where the Presbyterians and Dutch Calvinists were more numerous.[20]

It is difficult now to appreciate the bitterness of the Bishop's Controversy, and its importance in the early part of the revolutionary struggle. But, as John Adams wrote, 'If any gentleman supposes this controversy to be nothing to the present purpose, he is grossly mistaken. It [the scheme for a colonial episcopate] spread an universal alarm against the authority of Parliament. It excited a general and just apprehension, that bishops, and dioceses, and churches, and priests, and tithes, were to be imposed on us by Parliament. . . . If Parliament could tax us, they could establish the Church of England.'[21]

Or, consider the vehemence of Jonathan Mayhew's remarks on the subject; this from a man of liberal instincts and Unitarian leanings:

When we consider . . . what our forefathers suffred from the mitred lordly successors of the fishermen of Galilee, . . . when we reflect that one principal motive to their exchanging the fair cities, villages, and delightful fields of Britain for the then inhospitable

[20] A. L. Cross, *The Anglican Episcopate and the American Colonies* (London, 1902), p. 159; Trinterud, *American Tradition*, p. 342.
[21] Adams, *Works*, x. 185.

shores and deserts of America, was that they might here enjoy unmolested God's holy word and ordinances, without [bishops] . . . we cannot well think of that church's gaining ground here to any great degree. . . . Will they never let us rest in peace. . . . Is it not enough that they persecuted us out of the Old World? . . . What other New World remains as a sanctuary for us from . . . a flood of Episcopacy?[22]

In 1766 the Presbyterian and Connecticut Congregational clergy met together and agreed to co-operate in opposition to the appointment of an Anglican bishop for the colonies. The Anglicans had already met in convention and drawn up petitions praying for an American bishop. They commissioned the Reverend Thomas Chandler of Elizabeth, New Jersey, to write a popular pamphlet on the subject, and this led to a bitter pamphlet controversy between Chandler and the Reverend Charles Chauncy, the Congregational leader in Boston.[23]

Between 1767 and 1774 Myles Cooper, president of King's College in New York (which had been founded in 1754 as an Anglican school), made several journeys to Philadelphia and as far south as Virginia, to enlist the support of the Southern clergy in the Bishop's Controversy. There appears not to have been much enthusiasm for bishops among many of the Southern Episcopalians. The vestries in the South had prescriptive rights in the choice of ministers, and the churches seemed to the High Churchmen of the North half-Presbyterian in discipline and spirit. Even in Philadelphia William Smith was intent on preserving the local Anglican alliance with the Presbyterians against the Quakers, and did not want to alienate his allies by raising the ghost of Laud. Nevertheless, Smith did write a mild and judicious pamphlet in favour of an American bishop, and agreed to work with Cooper and the New Yorkers. South of Philadelphia Cooper found two zealous

[22] Jonathan Mayhew, *Observations on the Charter and Conduct of the Society for the Propagation of the Gospel in Foreign Parts* (Boston, 1763), pp. 155–6.   [23] Trinterud, *American Tradition*, pp. 237–9.

Anglicans in Jonathan Boucher and James Horrocks. Horrocks, the president of William and Mary College, and Boucher
were able to rally support for episcopacy among some of the
Virginia and Maryland clergy, respectively.[24]

From the first, the question of a bishop was inextricably en-
tangled in the larger political dispute. In 1766 the Presbyterian
Synod, meeting in New York, sent out a pastoral letter com-
bining the usual plea for religious revival with a fulsome exhor-
tation in favour of American liberty. It also passed a resolution
approving the repeal of the Stamp Act.[25] Thus the Presbyterians committed themselves to overt political activity, and
almost automatically forced the Anglicans into a defence of
British policies. This the Anglicans were not at all unwilling
to make, though the question of a bishop was still uppermost
in their minds. In one of his pamphlets Chandler, writing in
1766, blamed the negligence of the British government for the
rebellious spirit of the colonies. He wrote that 'if ye Interest of
the Church of England in America had been made a National
Concern from the beginning, by this time a general submission
in ye Colonies to ye Mother Country, in everything not sinful,
might have been expected, not only for wrath, but for con-
science' sake'.[26] Less judicious Churchmen asserted that Congregational and Presbyterian ministers were 'unceasingly
sounding the Yell of Rebellion in the Ears of an ignorant &
deluded People', and that one might 'as soon look for *Chastity*
in Brothels as for Loyalty among Independents'.[27] The New

[24] 'Letters of Jonathan Boucher', loc. cit. vii. 350; viii. 177; J. W. Lydekker,
The Life and Letters of Charles Inglis (London, 1936), pp. 117, 121–2; Cross,
Anglican Episcopate, passim.

[25] Trinterud, *American Tradition*, pp. 237–8.

[26] A. H. Hoyt, 'The Rev. Thomas Bradbury Chandler, D.D., 1726–1790',
New England Historical and Genealogical Register, xxvii. 233.

[27] Quoted, Miller, *American Revolution*, pp. 186, 195. In the Middle and
Southern Colonies 'Presbyterian' was always used to mean 'Congregationalist'
as well. Presbyterians were thought of as a local variety of 'New England
Independents'. As an example of this confusion in terminology, note the
remark of Alexander Mackrabie, writing from New York in 1768: 'The
Presbyterians should not be allowed to grow too great. They are all of
Republican Principles. The Bostonians are Presbyterians' (quoted, Trinterud,

York and New Jersey clergy wrote to the Society for the Propagation of the Gospel that 'Independence in Religion will naturally produce Republicans in the State'. And a Pennsylvania Anglican wrote that the Presbyterians were 'as averse to Kings, as they were in the Days of Cromwell'; they wanted to form 'a Republican Empire in America, being *Lords* and *Masters* themselves'.[28]

The campaign for an American episcopate failed to achieve its purpose, and the bitterness the controversy had aroused was absorbed into the general argument of the Revolution. In the course of the Bishop's Controversy, however, most of the Anglican clergy in the North had become an organized group of propagandists ready to work on Britain's behalf. That the Anglicans remained politically quiet between 1767 and 1774 seems to have been because they were waiting for a lead from the Tory politicians, or the British government. The secular atmosphere of the English colonies in America did not encourage clerical leadership, no longer even in New England. No group of parsons could safely assert the kind of leadership possible for the clergy in, say, French Canada. Accordingly the Anglicans waited, in growing bewilderment, for a movement of protest against the Revolution which they could join, but which they could not initiate.

American Tradition, p. 240). When Scots Presbyterians were meant, they were always called 'Scotch', and the Kirk of Scotland was regarded as quite different from the American Presbyterian Church. Thus Governor Martin of North Carolina explained to Lord Dartmouth that the American Presbyterians were 'not of the principles of the Church of Scotland, but like the people of New England, more of the leaven of the Independents' (ibid., p. 251).

The identification of Presbyterians with Congregationalists was not only politically useful, but may be justified in doctrine. L. J. Trinterud maintains that the 'genius of American Presbyterianism' was forged out of the union during the Great Awakening of New England Puritans settled in the Middle Colonies and a group of Scotch-Irish Presbyterians who had themselves 'been thoroughly imbued with the piety and views of English Puritanism' (ibid., p. 122). In other words, the Presbyterians in the Middle Colonies and South had acquired a New England outlook.

[28] Samuel Seabury, *Letters of a Westchester Farmer*, ed. C. H. Vance (White Plains, 1930), p. 3; Miller, *American Revolution*, p. 196.

It has already been suggested that one explanation for the comparative apathy of the Tories in the critical decade before 1774 lay in their lack of enthusiasm for the measures being pursued by the British government. Certainly this confusion as to whether their cause was their own or Britain's was an early handicap. As between the aims of the revolutionary movement and the claims of the British government, many Tories long held an attitude bordering on neutrality. In time, however, the Tories came to be inhibited less by doubt, than by their history, habits of mind, and a special plight.

Looking back on this period after the Revolution, most of the Tory writers were able to see a regular progression of events leading inevitably to revolution and independence. This seeming inevitability was a product of afterthought, however, since events as they happened did not possess the clarity they acquired in retrospect. At the time most of the Tories yielded to the common temptation of those who are satisfied with things as they are, to expect things to remain as they are. Like most anti-revolutionists, they found it difficult to regard the mere threat of revolution seriously. Thus at almost any time beween 1765 and 1774 it seemed to most of them that the revolutionary movement had nearly run its course, and that matters would shortly be as they had been before the Stamp Act.

Even when they were sure of their cause and sure that it needed their advocacy, the Tories were comparatively ineffective advocates.. They could not compete with the Whigs in organization, and they did not try to compete as propagandists. They distrusted innovations and were sceptical about reforms, so that while, in idle moments, many of them speculated on the constitutional problems facing the colonies, they failed utterly, during the years when they might have been listened to, to suggest a reasonable alternative to revolution. Apart from Galloway's plan for a union with Britain, discussed in a leisurely and academic way in Philadelphia, the Tory leaders avoided the basic issues of constitutional reform, and concentrated their attention on minor and peripheral matters:

the need for more (or fewer) British troops, or for higher salaries for judges, or for restrictions against town meetings. Most of the Tory office-holders seem to have been incapable of seeing beneath the superficial problems of administrative reform to the basic problems of constitutional reform.

Not only did they not develop and proclaim an agreed alternative to revolution, the Tories did not even consult among themselves except in the most haphazard and informal way. They developed no Committees of Correspondence, and very little political correspondence at all. Their letters remained the desultory and amiable communications of complacent gentlefolk. In fact, except for the Anglican parsons, the principal Tories in the different provinces, men like Hutchinson in Massachusetts, and Galloway in Pennsylvania, did not even know each other. It is odd to find some of them recording their first impressions of each other, in exile in London, long after the debate was over and their day was done.

Tories weakness

Most of all, the Tories were simply unable to cultivate public opinion, to form it and inform it. They showed not a trace of the skill with which, for example, Samuel Adams learned in these years to involve the reading public and the local politicians in a reciprocal catechism of alarms and grievances, of petitions and manifestoes echoed interminably back and forth, from committee to assembly, from assembly to committee, from the press to the public to the press. The Tories were, in fact, afraid of public opinion, afraid of men gathered together, even symbolically, in large numbers. They were afraid, for they felt weak. Here indeed is to be found the basic Tory inhibition during these years of argument, the real and compelling excuse for their apathy. They had ideas, beliefs, values, interests which they were afraid to submit to an American public for approval or rejection. And the weaker they felt themselves to be, the tighter became their allegiance to Britain. The closer they were bound to Britain, the less able were they to support effectively her cause or theirs. So, as the American quarrel with the British government grew more bitter and more deadly, the Tories

Tories did not develop Committees of Correspondence and had very little political correspondence.

began slowly, under the guise of loyalty, to sink into a helpless dependence on Britain, an attachment no longer voluntary but growing desperate, and as it became desperate, ceasing to be quite honourable.

CHAPTER II

The Essential Tory

THERE is no need to accept the Tory thesis that New England's ambitions were the guiding force of the Revolution in order to agree that the revolutionary movement developed more steadily and, after 1766 at least, more rapidly in New England than in the colonies to the south. In the Stamp Act crisis, it is true, Boston had produced no violence to match New York's, and the Virginia Resolves had gone further in challenging the authority of Parliament than the writings of Otis and Thacher. But from 1766 on, revolutionary activity seems to have been less intermittent and more purposeful in Massachusetts than elsewhere, partly perhaps because Boston had a more mature and less factious body politic than New York or Philadelphia.

The Massachusetts Convention of 1768 was a genuine revolutionary assembly, and its establishment a more serious challenge to British authority than any challenge made in the other colonies before 1774. It is true that, to the surprise and relief of the Boston Tories, the Convention failed to sanction armed resistance to Britain. Its formation was premature, and the royal government of Massachusetts appeared to resume its normal operation the following year. The significance of the Convention, however, lies more in the psychological than in the constitutional history of the Revolution. It was a revolutionary institution, overtly established and not suppressed, but only put aside until a more convenient time. From 1768 onwards Massachusetts was deeply involved in the crisis of sovereignty that spread to the colonies farther south only after the meeting of the First Continental Congress.[1]

[1] R. E. Brown, *Middle-Class Democracy and the Revolution in Massachusetts, 1691–1780* (Ithaca, 1955), pp. 252–4; J. C. Miller, 'The Massachusetts Convention: 1768', *New England Quarterly*, vii. 445–74.

The different pace of revolutionary development in New England and in the other colonies produced a certain tension which either the Tories or the British government might have exploited but which, fortunately for the course of the Revolution, neither did. Indeed, for the Tories, this difference in pace became a handicap. The New England Tories, weak to begin with, had for a long time to oppose the Revolution unsupported by their brethren to the south who, at least in the Middle Colonies, were in a much stronger position than they themselves. And eventually the Southern Tories found themselves opposing what was already an accomplished deed in New England, with the people there who could have supported them already beaten.

The plight and the failure of the New England Tories is exemplified in the career of Thomas Hutchinson. As chief justice, lieutenant-governor, and finally royal governor of Massachusetts, Hutchinson was for many years the most influential of the Tory office-holders. In New England he was venerated by lesser placemen and, if John Adams was correct, held in more than ordinary respect by people at large: 'Have not his countrymen', Adams wrote, 'loved, admired, revered, rewarded, nay, almost adored him? Have not ninety-nine in a hundred of them really thought him the greatest and best man in America?'[2] On the other hand, Samuel Adams wrote bitterly of Hutchinson that, 'It has been his principle from a boy that mankind are to be governed by the discerning few, and it has been ever since his ambition to be the hero of the few.'[3] There is, of course, no inherent contradiction between these appraisals: the hero of the 'discerning few' may also be, or may become, or may sometimes have been the hero of the many.

In the patriotic American and enthusiastic English Whig histories of the last century, Hutchinson, like many other Tory leaders, appears as a sinister and repelling character. Viewed

[2] Adams, *Works*, ii. 189.
[3] J. K. Hosmer, *Life of Thomas Hutchinson* (Boston, 1896), p. xx.

in the light of his times, however, or more properly in the light cast on his times from a little earlier in his century, he seems a perfectly straightforward, if limited, public man. He was in the lineal tradition of Massachusetts oligarchs, in the best tradition in fact, since he was not entirely content with oligarchy and longed for a genuine aristocracy. His life, until it began to be buffeted by revolution, was singularly well-ordered. When young, he had been a grave and steady student, delight-ing in history, learning French, a little Greek, and acquiring a 'relish for the Latin tongue' that lasted all his life. Although he himself eventually wrote placid history, he was not wholly unaware of the agonies of the past: he had wept for Charles I. He became a sober success in a number of fields: he was a prudent merchant, a well-loved husband and father, a lucid and honest lawyer, an incorruptible public servant, a faithful, laborious, scholarly man. He had a gift for clarity of thought and speech, so that jurymen used to tell each other when he rose to speak, 'Now we shall have something which we can understand.'[4]

Hutchinson's public reputation was established in 1749 when he was influential in restoring the value of Massachusetts currency by a ruthless repudiation of depreciated paper. Much as the 'discerning few'—in this case chiefly the creditor class—admired him for this, it cost him his seat in the General Court, and he found it afterwards both necessary and profitable to pursue his career by appointment.[5]

For all his virtues—his rationality, his sobriety, his modera-tion—partly in fact because of his virtues, Hutchinson was a man singularly ill-equipped either to lead or oppose a revolu-tion. His conservatism was not active and constructive like that of some of the other Tory leaders; it was passive, instinc-tive, and narrowly defensive. Faced with a radical proposal for dealing with a matter of policy, it was Hutchinson's habit not to make a counter-proposal, but simply to criticize the offending plan. In argument he sometimes showed insight and

---

[4] Ibid., pp. xv, 2–3.   [5] Ibid., pp. 25–36.

always he showed intelligence, but he lacked sympathy. He was unable to recognize and respect the depth of other men's grievances, but tended rather to dismiss them as irrational. Although he appeared tolerant and judicious, in him these qualities seem the result of disinterest rather than of deep understanding. In troubled times, when he was asked not to judge, but to act, his detachment was to prove a fatal handicap.

Although in 1765 Hutchinson had vigorously opposed the Stamp Act, he shortly became alarmed at the violence of the popular opposition to the Act, a violence marked in his own case by the destruction of his house by a mob. He later observed that the revolt of the colonies should have been dated from the Stamp Act crisis rather than from any succeeding event. The committees appointed to supervise opposition to the Stamp Act, and also the Stamp Act Congress itself, were, he wrote, 'confederacies to limit the supreme authority' of Parliament. After 1765, he maintained, Britain might have been able to restore her authority in America, but she could no longer simply exercise it.

As early as 1766 Hutchinson was emphasizing, in his letters to England, the corrosive effect on British authority of the successful defiance of Parliament the year before. He noted that the spirit of independence was making rapid progress. He described, with more apprehension than irony, what he called the actual constitution of Massachusetts. The lowest branch of government, he wrote, 'partly legislative, partly executive', consisted of the 'rabble of the town of Boston, headed by one Mackintosh'. These were partly controlled by 'a superior set of master-masons and carpenters', who condescended in matters of importance to be directed by a committee of merchants. The apex of this informal constitution was the town meeting, where 'mob-high eloquence' prevailed. The governor, Council, and House of Representatives, he wrote, were almost equally unable to resist the new government, even though he thought people at large were still loyal to the old constitution. Like Governor Bernard, Hutchinson urged the government in

Clarify Constitutional issues—

London to give a precise, constitutional definition to the connexion between Britain and the colonies. The nature and degree of American dependence ought to 'be settled, known, and admitted'.[6]

By 1768 Hutchinson observed that the claim to independence of Parliament was almost universally made in Boston. The King's authority, he wrote, was still admitted, even exalted, but he saw no reason why the royal authority might not be denied as easily as the parliamentary, since the Crown's right was based on an Act of Parliament. He wrote to Richard Jackson urging that Parliament make a declaration recognizing the colonies' internal autonomy, and promising not to exercise the supreme legislative power except for such imperial purposes as the regulation of trade and defence. His hopes of tranquillity, Hutchinson said, rested entirely on the possibility that his countrymen might eventually be convinced, first, that Parliament would not give up its authority, and second, that it would exercise it prudently.[7]

Townshend Duties imprudent

Whatever hopes of effective British action Hutchinson still had in 1768 were dampened by the Townshend Duties, which he thought imprudent, and the Non-Importation Agreements in response to the duties which, along with the establishment of the Massachusetts Convention, he thought marked a far step in the achievement of revolution. It was at this time that Hutchinson wrote to Jackson that 'there must be an abridgment of what are called English liberties', a statement which was later cited by his enemies to prove he was an apologist for tyranny. More precisely, he believed that while in an arbitrarily ruled state, a passion for liberty might have a good effect, in an already free society like America a liberal creed could lead only to chaos, 'unless there be some external power to restrain it'. Hutchinson thought that while independence might be desirable at some later date when American institutions had matured, its premature establishment would lead to

Apologist for Tyranny

[6] Hosmer, *Life of Hutchinson*, pp. 103–4, 120–2.
[7] Ibid., p. 137.

mob tyranny.[8] In hoping that Britain might serve as the 'external power' to restrain his countrymen, Hutchinson was, of course, confessing the weakness of the Tory position in New England.

Hutchinson's real and persistent aim seems simply to have been to go back to the peaceful days before 1763, to see a return to things as they were. He gradually became convinced, however, that this retreat would have to be forced on the colonies by the British government. When the Ministry had first attempted to tax the colonies, Hutchinson had advised against it. By 1770, however, he had decided that British authority was too much despised for it ever to recover through judicious disuse, and he advised forceful measures to restore its vigour. By this time, to Hutchinson's dismay, the British government had decided to 'let all controversy subside, and by degrees suffer matters to return to their old channel'. The Ministry were chagrined at Hutchinson's 'officiousness' and ignored his pleas for action as their predecessors had ignored his pleas for caution.[9]

Hutchinson persisted, almost desperately, in urging the government to act. He wrote to London that the time of grace for Britain was running out, that it would become more and more difficult to restore Parliament's authority, that they did not live 'in the Commonwealth of Plato'. 'It is not now time', he wrote, 'to grudge at a small expense to save the whole Colony.' The urgency of his pleas contrasts strangely, however, with the triviality of the action he sought. Apart from advising the arrest of the radical leaders of the town of Boston, he seems to have made no serious recommendation except that the jurisdiction of the Boston Town Meeting be restricted to town affairs, and that only qualified voters be allowed to attend meetings. As matters stood, he said, the town meeting was dominated by professional radicals, often non-voters and even non-residents, people who 'if met together upon

[8] Hosmer, *Life of Hutchinson*, pp. 143–4.   [9] Ibid., pp. 251–2.

another occasion, would be properly called a mob'. Such an assembly as this, he wrote indignantly, was 'not even a democracy'.[10]

Proposals for fundamental constitutional change seem never to have interested Hutchinson. No reform, he insisted, would be of any use until the essential question of sovereignty was settled. Either Parliament's authority extended to America, or it did not. If it did, there was no need to change the constitution. If it did not, there was no point in trying to. 'All the present disorder in the Colonies', he wrote, was owing to British neglect in having allowed the sense of the supremacy of Parliament gradually to 'go off from the minds of the people'.[11]

In his grasp of the essential psychological conditions for an acceptance of British authority, Hutchinson was wiser than Tory constitutionalists like Galloway and William Smith. In his analysis of the constitutional problems of Anglo-American relations, however, he fell far below them. In 1770 William Smith wrote to him that nothing could restore the authority of government in America but a 'Lord Lieutenant and an American Parliament'. Hutchinson thought this was impracticable. His New England particularism was offended and he suggested instead (as Governor Shirley had done at the Albany Congress) three regional governments: one for New England and Nova Scotia, one for the Middle Colonies and Virginia, and one for the South. These three provinces might, he thought, be put under the supervision of a governor-general. If any such plan were adopted the opportunity might be taken to make the individual colonial constitutions as nearly uniform as possible, and to strengthen the executive authority. Parliament's authority over the whole could also be defined clearly. That he was not at all sure any such scheme would work is suggested by Hutchinson's rather vague endorsement of his own plan: 'Be this as it may, it is certainly best to make some

stir. To be still only gives time for the principles of independence to spread and to be confirmed.'[12]

Hutchinson's hopes rose during the period of calm which
spread over the colonies in the early 1770's. The repeal of the
Townshend Duties in 1770, except for the tax on tea, had contributed to the collapse of the non-importation movement. The
economic basis of the quarrel with Britain, especially the merchants' quarrel, was weakened at the same time by the revival
of prosperity. The merchants began to desert the revolutionary
movement, especially outside New England; even in Boston,
John Hancock, the linchpin of the alliance between the merchants and the radicals, broke with Samuel Adams. Hutchinson wrote hopefully that the merchants were beginning to find
the 'Democratick Tyranny' of a 'lawless banditti' oppressive.
Following the Boston Massacre, Hutchinson had tried to resign
as acting-governor, and had written to John Pownall that the
'spirit of anarchy . . . in Boston is more than I am able to cope
with'. But as the months passed and there were no new disorders, he took heart and agreed to accept the governorship,
succeeding Bernard, who had returned to England. He was
pleased with the apparent public approval of his appointment
as governor, although he noted that, among the congratulatory
addresses he received, there were not the usual felicitations
from the House of Representatives and the Congregational
ministers of Boston.[13]

The strong conservative reaction in the legislative session of
May 1771 added to Hutchinson's confidence. He observed with
quiet satisfaction that Samuel Adams's efforts to transform the
House of Representatives into a revolutionary assembly had
broken down. He took comfort in Adams's much-reduced

[12] Hosmer, *Life of Hutchinson*, pp. 168–9; William Smith, *Historical
Memoirs from 16 March, 1763 to 9 July, 1776 of William Smith*, ed. W. H. W.
Sabine (New York, 1956), p. 236. Smith should not be confused with the
Reverend William Smith of Philadelphia.

[13] Hosmer, *Life of Hutchinson*, pp. 189, 192, 203; A. M. Schlesinger, *The
Colonial Merchants and the American Revolution* (New York, 1918),
pp. 254–5.

majority in the elections of 1772, and observed that the news-papers were beginning to print Tory letters and articles.[14] Viewed in the light of the whole revolutionary struggle, this tranquil period in 1771 and 1772 was like the bright calm at the centre of a hurricane. But Hutchinson, despite his remark that 'it is certainly best to make some stir', succumbed to the Tory yearning for peace, and basked in the sun of these quiet days.

The American Tories shared the universal tendency of public men to interpret political events in personal terms, a tendency strengthened in their case by oligarchical habits of mind. The Tory leaders had been accustomed all their political lives to know the men in their own provinces who held office or wanted to hold office. They thought of politics largely in terms of what men or families should be advanced, placated, or kept down. In all the American colonies the party politics of the day were dominated by family interest and personal favour. It was natural as the revolutionary movement grew for the Tories to think of their opponents in terms of personality rather than principle. Here the first thing that impressed the Tory oligarchs was the personal obscurity of many of the revolutionary leaders. 'Men whom nobody knows', were becoming all too well known. Old Governor Shirley's concern in this regard was characteristic: 'Mr. Cushing I knew, and Mr. Hancock I knew, but where the devil this brace of Adamses came from, I know not.'[15]

Hutchinson was more perceptive than most of his fellows, yet even he, in his less thoughtful moments, found the dynamics of the revolutionary movement in the envy and ambition of the revolutionary leaders. The 'brace of Adamses' in particular, seemed to him to have caused much trouble. 'We have not been so quiet these five years', he wrote in 1771, '. . . if it were not for two or three Adamses, we should do well enough. I don't know how to account for the obstinacy

[14] Hosmer, *Life of Hutchinson*, pp. 219, 224.
[15] Adams, *Works*, ii. 233.

of one, who seemed to me, when he began life, to promise well. The other never appeared different from what he does at present.'[16]

John Adams's naturally good judgement had been warped, as Hutchinson saw it, by his inordinate and frustrated ambition. 'His ambition', Hutchinson wrote of Adams, 'was without bounds, and he has acknowledged to his acquaintance that he could not look with complacency upon any man who was in possession of more wealth, more honours, or more knowledge than himself.' Hutchinson's *bête noire*, however, was Samuel Adams, the 'Master of the Puppets'. Although, he wrote, it was difficult to decide which of the Adamses laboured under a stronger feeling of personal neglect or injury, there was no question that Samuel Adams was the greater villain. 'A great pretended zeal for liberty, and a most inflexible natural temper', he told George III, had given Adams his importance. And in his *History* he wrote of Adams that, 'long practice caused him ... to acquire a talent of artfully and fallaciously insinuating into the minds of his readers a prejudice against the characters of all whom he attacked ... the prevailing principle of the party, that the end justified the means, probably quieted the remorse he must have felt, from robbing men of their characters'.

Compared with the Adamses, the other leaders of the Revolution in New England seemed negligible to Hutchinson. He dismissed Hancock as an empty-headed fellow whose 'ruling passion was a fondness for popular applause'. 'His natural powers', he wrote acidly of Hancock, 'were moderate, and had been very little improved by study.' James Otis was, in Hutchinson's view, a thoughtful and well-intentioned man who simply went insane.[17]

While Hutchinson regarded his worst opponents as indigent demagogues, they, of course, thought of him as a vain and

[16] Hosmer, *Life of Hutchinson*, p. 192.
[17] Thomas Hutchinson, *The History of the Colony and Province of Massachusetts Bay*, ed. L. S. Mayo (3 vols., Cambridge, 1936), iii. 212–15; id., *Diary*, i. 167.

assuming oligarch. They dwelt with bitter relish on the family allegiance between the Hutchinsons and the Olivers, and pointed out that when Hutchinson was governor, his brother-in-law, Andrew Oliver, was lieutenant-governor; his brother, Foster, justice of the Common Pleas; his son, Thomas, a newly made judge of probate; and his daughter's father-in-law, Peter Oliver, chief justice of the province. There was undoubtedly an element of truth in John Adams's conviction that Hutchinson was a Tory because he wanted to be an earl, just as there probably was in Hutchinson's belief that Adams was a revolutionist because he had not been made a sheriff. But as explanations of motive, both beliefs are gravely insufficient.

In the years between 1771 and 1773 Hutchinson came quietly to despair of any effective British action to destroy the revolutionary movement, while at the same time he continued to hope that the trend towards independence might lose its force, and the Revolution die a natural death. He continued, it is true, regularly to recommend to the government in England that it somehow re-establish its authority in America. His specific recommendations remained almost absurdly limited, however: to his earlier suggestions that the radical leaders of Boston be arrested and town meetings be restricted, he added a plea for the withdrawal of British troops, whom he had discovered at the time of the Boston Massacre to be an embarrassment rather than a support to the government. 'Troops', he wrote, 'can be useful in case of actual rebellion only, when civil government ceases, and the military is at liberty to act independent.'[18]

In the political life of Massachusetts Hutchinson continued to 'stand absolutely alone', or to believe, not without a certain pride, that he stood alone. He did nothing to encourage, or create, or finance a Tory party in the province. At most, he worked privately to keep uncommitted towns outside Boston from joining in revolutionary activity. He also did nothing to discover grounds of common action with men similarly placed

[18] Hutchinson, *History*, iii. 233; Hosmer, *Life of Hutchinson*, pp. 230–1.

in other colonies. His political correspondence, he thought, was properly with the government in London, and properly should remain so. While Samuel Adams worked systematically to develop the Committees of Correspondence into an effective instrument of revolution, Hutchinson did nothing to expand his own contacts in the other colonies, and seems to have remained ignorant even of the names of men in New York or Pennsylvania who shared his opinions. Indeed, Hutchinson's initial view of the Committees of Correspondence illustrates his lack of a sense of political organization, as well as of any sense of the importance of cultivating public opinion. 'Such a foolish scheme', he wrote of Adams's committees, 'that they must necessarily make themselves ridiculous.' Even when, early in 1773, he revised his opinion of the Committees of Correspondence and wrote, 'the proceeding is to be regarded as very dangerous', he did nothing either to hinder or emulate Adams.[19]

From the early months of 1773 onwards Hutchinson realized that his cause and position were deteriorating. He reported that the Committees of Correspondence had succeeded in getting resolutions passed in all the Massachusetts towns denying Parliament's authority in general terms. He felt that the movement towards independence had secured its gains and was ready to go forward whenever it could find a proper grievance. He wrote that he had hitherto kept much of rural Massachusetts from joining the Boston radicals, but he felt the radicals were now gaining strength in the whole province. His despair and his inflexible passivity are clear in his estimate of his situation: 'Nothing more is in my power than to stand my ground against a constant opposition, and now and then to throw something before them to catch at and direct them from their main object, tearing the constitution to pieces.'[20]

To Hutchinson there was no question what constitution the radicals were tearing to pieces. It was the British constitution,

[19] Hosmer, *Life of Hutchinson*, pp. 235, 243.   [20] Ibid., p. 250.

not the unwritten British constitution rooted in natural rights which the revolutionists still spoke of with veneration, but the historical constitution, as established finally in 1688, complete with the sovereignty of Parliament. Nothing, no argument, no plan, no stratagem, ever led Hutchinson to deny for a moment the sovereignty of Parliament. 'I know of no line', he wrote, 'that can be drawn between the supreme authority of Parliament and the total independence of the colonies.' That he might have been especially well placed to discover a middle ground between these two mutually exclusive claims was a thought that, if it ever occurred to him at all, Hutchinson rejected firmly.

Early in 1773, realizing it might well be his last chance as governor, Hutchinson presented an elaborate, learned, and careful defence of the sovereignty of Parliament in the form of several speeches to the House of Representatives and Council of Massachusetts. Here was no attempt, such as Galloway and William Smith were to make, to reconcile the claims of Britain and America, or to enlarge the British constitution to include the colonies on equal terms with Britain. Hutchinson's constitutional argument was stiff, narrow, uncompromising, and, given its first assumptions, impeccably logical. He began by observing that Parliament had exercised the supreme authority in the colony for more than a century, and that except for the period of anarchy just before the Restoration, its right to do so had never been questioned. Since, by the common opinion, there could be only one supreme power in a state, the colony governments, he reasoned, must be inferior corporations, although possessing more general powers than municipal corporations in England. As to the right of representation in Parliament, Hutchinson maintained that the colonists had lost this right by leaving England, but they had not become foreigners, or in any way been exempted from obedience to the laws of England.

At one point Hutchinson came to grips with the central argument of the revolutionists, the question of natural rights.

To him, however, this problem presented no difficulties. 'Natural rights', he said, were forfeited to any government, and to use an argument based on such rights against a particular form of government was simply meaningless. Similarly, it was neither reasonable nor permissible to make objections to particular acts of government into general disavowals of the government's *right* to govern. Hutchinson concluded by inviting the Council and the House to agree with his interpretation, or alternatively, to define their point of view for him, so that he might be convinced, or be given an opportunity to convince them. He hoped, he wrote drily, to settle the question one way or another.

The Council made a moderate reply to Hutchinson's speech, written chiefly by James Bowdoin. It denied the validity of Hutchinson's concept of 'supreme authority' which the Council took to mean 'unlimited authority'; the Council thought there was none such, except God's. They freely admitted Parliament's 'supreme regulatory authority', but denied that Parliament had the right to tax the colonies, since the colonies were unrepresented, and representation had always been associated with taxation in England.

Hutchinson answered the Council by noting with approval their disavowal of independence; he suggested that, 'upon more mature deliberation', it should be clear to them that it was better to doubt the expediency of particular Acts of Parliament than to try to limit Parliament's taxing authority while admitting its supremacy in all other matters.

The reply of the House of Representatives to Hutchinson denied entirely that the authority of Parliament had ever extended outside the realm of England. The colonies, therefore, owed allegiance to the King alone. While the Council had agreed with Hutchinson in deploring riots and disorder, the House denied there had been any disorder. The House's reply was uncompromising in tone; significantly the word 'justice' was passed over in favour of the word 'equity': 'by what authority, in reason or equity . . . ?'

Hutchinson told the House that it made a serious error in not distinguishing between the Crown of England and the kings of England in their personal capacities. Only the Crown, of which Parliament was a part, could make grants or charters, such as the Massachusetts Charter. He reminded the House that the Charter itself had originally exempted the colony from customs duties for twenty-one years, thus implying Parliament's right to levy such duties after that time. Hutchinson denied that Parliament had no authority outside the 'ancient territorial realm'; he cited Acts for regulating affairs in Ireland, Wales, and Calais when they were unrepresented in Parliament, and similar Acts for the Channel Isles, which were still unrepresented. He noted that the accession of William and Mary had been proclaimed in New England by virtue of an Act of Parliament, not by action of any colony, and that other Acts of Parliament had been accepted without question in New England for many years.

The House of Representatives made a long reply to Hutchinson's second speech, full of legalistic refinements, but evading Hutchinson's specific arguments. The point of the House's reply was that if Acts of Parliament had been obeyed in the colonies, it had been because it was convenient to do so, not because there had been any obligation to obey them. The chief effect of this exchange of views between Hutchinson and the two Houses was to drive the radicals close to making a premature claim of complete independence. This may have been what Hutchinson wanted, for its effect on opinion in England, as well as on conservatives in Massachusetts.[21]

By this time Hutchinson observed numerous signs of the Revolution's further advance in New England. The Massachusetts House of Representatives had assumed the name of 'His Majesty's Commons'; its debates had become 'parliamentary debates'; Acts of Parliament were now 'Acts of the British Parliament'; even the Town House had become the

[21] Hutchinson's speeches to the House and Council may be found in Hosmer, *Life of Hutchinson*, Appendix B, pp. 363 ff.

'State House'. To all this, Hutchinson wrote, he offered no objection in the hope there would be no further grievance for the radicals to exploit. He continued to hold a lingering belief that the revolutionary movement was a disease that might run its course, a hysterical and feverish distemper of a kind not unusual in New England society. He wrote that 'the deception cannot last longer than it did in the time of the witchcraft. Truth at worst will finally prevail.'[22]

The Boston Tea Party caught Hutchinson off guard. Revolutionary enthusiasm had seemed at a low ebb in Boston in the autumn of 1773, and Hutchinson wrote afterwards that he had just been congratulated by an observant friend on the 'fair prospect of being a popular governor', when news arrived of the radicals' plans to demonstrate against the tea tax. To Hutchinson the Tea Party was a criminal as well as a revolutionary act. He registered the formal abhorrence of the royal government at the deed by having the attorney-general lay the known facts about the affair before a grand jury. The grand jury refused to take any action and, Hutchinson wrote, 'There was not a justice of the peace, sheriff, constable, or peace officer in the province, who would venture to take cognizance of any breach of law, against the general bent of the people.'[23]

The Tea Party led to the abrupt cessation of Hutchinson's public career. He was replaced as governor by General Thomas Gage, who was sent out with 10,000 troops to pacify New England. The Boston Port Act closed the port of Boston to commerce, while another Act of Parliament prohibited town meetings without the prior consent of the governor, and strengthened the governor's power of appointment. Hutchinson decided that his immediate usefulness in Boston was at an end, and applied for 'discretionary leave' to go to England. When he left for England in June 1774 he received respectful addresses from the conservative merchants and gentlemen of Boston and the other towns, but the attitude of the radicals

[22] Hutchinson, *History*, iii. 296-7; Hosmer, *Life of Hutchinson*, p. 285.
[23] Ibid., pp. 300-3; Hutchinson, *History*, iii. 314-15.

was expressed succinctly by John Andrews, who wrote that he was a 'tool of tyrants' and a 'damn'd *arch traitor*'.[24]

Hutchinson's stated reasons for leaving America were, that he felt he could do no more in New England, that he hoped he might be able to conciliate the Ministry, obtain the repeal of the Port Act, and take part in any general settlement which might be made between Britain and the colonies. The revolutionists assumed simply that he had fled. In a sense he probably had done so. He was a proud, sensitive man, more concerned than most of the Tory office-holders to have the good opinion of his neighbours. For nearly ten years he had tried to uphold the right as he knew it in an atmosphere growing steadily more hostile. He was tired of being the chief symbol of an alien tyranny in his own town. Although his political convictions seem never to have wavered, he was at times genuinely puzzled at the widening gulf between him and his fellow Bostonians. 'Either my brain is turned', he wrote once, 'or the brains of most of the people about me are so.' Another time he complained that 'a gentleman does not meet with what used to be common civility', and in 1772 he wrote to former Governor Pownall, 'If you was now in America you would be sick of it in a week and leave it.'[25]

In addition, however, to being glad to leave an environment which had long ceased to be congenial and was now becoming intolerable, Hutchinson seemed seriously to have believed he could influence British policy. And it did not occur to him now, any more than it had done earlier, that the final decisions as to America's future could be made anywhere but in London.

Hutchinson's limitations are obvious and grave, though not nearly so grave as the nineteenth-century historians made out. His own judgement of himself was too gentle, however: all he could bring himself to say was that he 'was, perhaps, in some degree biassed by an attachment to that form of government

---

[24] 'Letters of John Andrews', Massachusetts Historical Society, *Proceedings*, 1st series, viii. 328; Hosmer, *Life of Hutchinson*, pp. 312–16.

[25] Ibid., pp. 134–5, 189, 346.

under which he had always lived'.[26] His bias took the form, at
its worst, of an obstinate adherence to the claims of a decaying
oligarchy. More than that, he was arrogant. He was too genuine
a New Englander not to feel some sympathy for the aspirations
of his fellow countrymen; he was convinced of the inevitability,
perhaps even the desirability, of ultimate American independence. But he refused flatly to seek any compromise with
those whose visions of America's future differed at all from his
own. He insisted that the destiny of the colonies must be left
in the hands of himself and others of his class, supported by
the British government—that 'external power', as external
to Hutchinson as it was to Samuel Adams. It was wrong for
Hutchinson, as it is always wrong, to believe that the formal
legitimacy of the governors was a tolerable substitute for the
consent of the governed.

If he was an oligarch, however, and would have been a complacent oligarch had the times allowed him to be, Hutchinson
was an upright and principled oligarch. He was untainted by
the opportunism and guile that disfigured some of the Tory
leaders in the Middle Colonies. By his resolute refusal to concern himself with public opinion, to cultivate it, to manipulate
it, or even to listen to it, Hutchinson at least avoided the sub-
terfuges and indignities that often cling to democratic politicians, especially when they are conservatives. He was that most
uncommon of American public men, an honest conservative,
pretending neither to love the people, nor even to represent
them, but claiming only, albeit presumptuously, to govern
them dutifully. To be sure, he always wanted the approval of
his countrymen, but he wanted it for doing what his judgement, not theirs, told him to do; 'I wish for the good opinion
of my countrymen', he wrote, 'if I could acquire it without
disturbing the peace of my own mind.'[27]

Although he would doubtless have denied it, Hutchinson
stood in a tradition: not, as he thought, one of faithful service

---

[26] Hutchinson, *History*, iii. 232–3.
[27] Hosmer, *Life of Hutchinson*, p. 334.

to the Crown, but in the authentic Puritan tradition. He was perhaps the last of the New England aristocrats, the true descendant of Governor Winthrop. But in his day the social and theological basis of the old aristocracy was gone; instead of Winthrop's just and terrible God, there was, for Hutchinson, only the rather absurd figure of George III. This was his most serious public weakness, that the real nature and origin of the authority he claimed, the authority of the Puritan *élite*, had vanished and could not be resurrected, for sake of convenience, in the shape of the British government.

Since he insisted on being a public figure, it is in this character that Hutchinson must be chiefly remembered, and remembered as a failure. He failed either to hold the confidence of his fellow Americans, much as he wanted it, or to uphold successfully the authority of Britain. He was ideally placed to lead the American Tories in a conservative, a conserving, movement against the violence and provincialism of the Revolution, yet he did not lead. He succeeded in one thing only, in maintaining his dignity and integrity under trying circumstances. This was, of course, no little thing to do, for as Hutchinson himself wrote once, with characteristic dispassion: 'It requires no small degree of fortitude to stand against a popular torrent, when it runs with violence.'[28]

[28] Hutchinson, *History*, iii. 143.

CHAPTER III

The Moderate Men

THE leaders of the American Revolution were remarkable, among revolutionists, for their durability. New men, it is true, appeared from time to time; some of the old dropped from view; but there were none of the violent and successive over-turns of leadership that characterize other revolutions. Some of the men whose first public appearance is in the revolutionary committees of the 1760's, who attend the First Continental Congress together, and who hold office during the Revolutionary War, may still be seen as national leaders a quarter of a century later, and even, like John Adams and Thomas Jefferson, be found busily occupied with public affairs a half-century after Governor Hutchinson had departed from Boston. This continuity of leadership was a part of the Revolution's strength and a symbol of its coherence.

Among the men who opposed the Revolution, however, a lack of continuity in direction is almost equally striking. The Tories never produced any truly national leaders at all, and after 1773 their local leaders changed almost from year to year. Thus before 1774 opposition to the revolutionary movement was led mainly by royal officials and was centred in New England. With Hutchinson's flight from Boston in the spring of 1774, official opposition to the Revolution in New England virtually collapsed, and the centre of Tory activity moved to the Middle Colonies. Here, except for Governor William Franklin in New Jersey, the most influential conservatives were not royal officials, but rather a few seasoned politicians who thought of themselves as 'moderate men'. Two of the most important of these men, Galloway in Pennsylvania and William Smith in New York, had habitually been in opposition rather than in office.

It is clear that, by the summer of 1774, the Revolution had gone much further in New England than in the provinces to the south. There were, of course, men in New York, Philadelphia, and even Charleston as hostile to British claims as Samuel Adams himself, but their influence was held down by local conservatives, men of a class which in Boston generally supported the opposition to Britain. The disinclination of many political leaders outside New England to support the revolutionary movement seems to be accountable not so much to kinder feelings towards Parliament's authority as to the graver social tensions in these colonies. With the exception of Virginia, none of the Middle or Southern Colonies formed societies as homogeneous as that of New England. The hostility between town and countryside, notable in New England only in the case of Newport, was sharp in New York, Pennsylvania, and South Carolina. The division between rich and poor was bitter in the towns of the Middle Colonies as well as in parts of the rural South. Rivalry between the new settlements of the Piedmont and the areas of older settlement near the coast was more intense in almost all the other colonies than it was in New England. There was also a conflict, particularly evident in New York and Pennsylvania, between evenly matched religious groups, especially between the Anglicans and the Presbyterians. Finally there was the mistrust, almost unknown in New England, between English colonists and those of different nationality—Ulstermen, Dutchmen, Germans, and Scots. These stresses helped to give the Carolinas and Middle Colonies a political life more factious and uneasy, perhaps less democratic, certainly less mature, than that of New England. The solid consent of a New England community, held together by a common Church and culture, could not readily be obtained in the scattered and heterogeneous settlements of these colonies.

It is true that Virginia, although afflicted with a discontented frontier area and a growing religious division, was still largely free from the disunities of the neighbouring provinces and formed a comparatively old and stable community. And eventually Virginia was to support the Revolution, or rather her own revolution, with a unanimity perhaps almost as great as that of Massachusetts. But in the direct challenge to British authority which had led in Boston to the landing of an army of pacification, Virginia had taken little part. Even radical Virginians continued in 1774 to discuss constitutional issues between Britain and the colonies in terms which had been abandoned for years in New England. The crux of the difference in attitude between Virginia and Massachusetts may have lain in the difference between rebellion and revolution. Virginians were not unwilling to be rebels, to fight the old Whig fight against the most modest claims of a central government, but they seem to have had little initial desire to be revolutionists, to want to substitute a new American sovereignty for the old sovereignty of Britain. The New Englanders certainly felt they could depend on Virginia's support only if British aggression, in fact or appearance, were allowed to determine the course of events. Meanwhile, during the critical summer of 1774, Virginia remained strangely quiet, as she was again to do in a similar time of crisis almost a century later.

With New England intransigent, Virginia hesitant, and the Carolinas remote and divided, it is understandable that the initiative for a negotiated settlement of the dispute with Britain should have come from the troubled but cosmopolitan Middle Colonies of New York and Pennsylvania, where resentment towards Britain merely shared a place in a spectrum of other fears and alarms. In New York several events during the earlier years of the dispute with Britain had alienated conservatives from their original support of radical measures in opposition to Parliament. Perhaps the first was the Stamp Act Riot in November 1765, when a mob, larger and less disciplined than the Boston mob, had torn through the town of New York, threatening less discriminate violence than it actually committed, but exposing none the less the naked inability of the propertied classes to maintain order. Another was the sobering commercial blow New York suffered during the enforcement of the Non-Importation Agreement in 1769, when the town's trade with England had been cut more sharply than Boston's or Philadelphia's. In 1770, after the repeal of the Townshend Duties, most of the New York merchants had abandoned the Sons of Liberty and had made peace, commercially, with England. A sudden solicitude for law and order began to affect practical politicians like James Duane, who wrote that, 'Every good man wishes to see Order restored, and the government resume its due weight.' When, in the elections of 1770, the Sons of Liberty were heavily defeated, the New York mob seemed 'muzzl'd at last', and the old Tory lieutenant-governor, Cadwallader Colden, was able to observe cheerfully that 'Government has renewed its strength'.[1]

The conservative reaction of 1770 in New York was, of course, part of a more general moderation of the dispute with Britain, the effects of which Hutchinson had noted even in Boston. In New York, however, the conservatives had learned their lesson well, and had worked systematically to prevent a radical revival. Even the Tea Act, which pushed Boston into open conflict with the imperial government, failed to shake the restraining hold of the New York conservatives on the revolutionary movement there. The Sons of Liberty did manage to dump a consignment of East India Company tea into New York harbour, but only to the decorous strains of *God Save the King*, played by a band on shore. And the unwillingness of the New York merchants to see mere politics interfere with trade is clear in this remark of a New Yorker to a friend in London: 'I heartily wish that an end were put to all disputes between us . . . for whilst these contentions last, the merchants of your city must feel the effects of it as well as us.'[2]

---

[1] E. B. O'Callaghan, ed., *Documents Relative to the Colonial History of the State of New York* (Albany, 1857), viii. 199, 213, 217, hereafter cited as *N.Y. Col. Doc.*; C. L. Becker, *The History of Political Parties in the Province of New York, 1760–1776* (Madison, 1909), pp. 83–93; E. P. Alexander, *A Revolutionary Conservative: James Duane of New York* (New York, 1938), p. 96; Schlesinger, *Colonial Merchants*, pp. 254–5; Miller, *American Revolution*, p. 309.

[2] Peter Force, ed., *American Archives: Consisting of a Collection of*

The New York gentry, however, were concerned with more than trade: they were afraid of social revolution. 'Believe me, sir,' Gouverneur Morris wrote, 'freedom and religion are only watchwords.' Such words, he explained, had been harmless enough so long as the shepherds had kept the dictionary of the day and given them their meaning, but now the sheep had got out of hand, the 'mobility grow dangerous to the gentry, and how to keep them down is the question'. Morris decided that if the dispute with Britain were not settled, New York would come under the domination of a riotous mob. 'It is in the interest of all men, therefore,' he concluded, 'to seek for reunion with the parent State.'[3] It was this apprehension of class struggle that cleared the minds of the New York oligarchs when men like themselves in other colonies were still excited with ideas of liberty.

Afraid as they were of revolution, the New York conservatives might have forthrightly opposed Boston and the local Sons of Liberty, and attempted to negotiate directly with the British government for concessions. This, however, might have led to the social conflict the Tories most feared, and might also have exposed to the British the weakness of the local oligarchy. For if they were afraid of the Sons of Liberty, the New York conservatives still hoped to use them as a weapon against British regulation, as indeed they had done for years. Consequently they decided, despite the growing heat of the quarrel with Britain, to continue trying to work with and restrain the radicals. In order to reduce radical influence in the New York Committee, the conservatives, with characteristic skill and guile, expanded the radical Committee of Twenty-Five into the Committee of Fifty-One, of whom twenty-seven were dependably prudent; 'men of sense, coolness, and property' elbowed 'flam-

---

Authentick Records, State Papers, Debates and Letters (Washington, 1837–53), 4th series, i. 299–302, cited hereafter as 4 *Am. Arch.* for 4th series, and 5 *Am. Arch.* for 5th series; H. M. Morais, 'The Sons of Liberty in New York', in *The Era of the American Revolution*, ed. R. B. Morris (New York, 1939), pp. 284–6; Becker, *Political Parties*, pp. 109–10.

[3] 4 *Am. Arch.* i. 342–3.

ing patriots' into the background, but not into overt opposition. It was this carefully diluted committee which, in May 1774, received a request from the Boston Committee for absolute non-intercourse with England.[4]

Now for the first time the New Yorkers were forced to consider seriously, not a merely provincial, but an American political problem, the problem, in fact, of finding an alternative to war and revolution. They responded by proposing what, with better preparation and more genuine statesmanship, might even have provided a solution to their problem. Recalling the apparent success of the Congress of 1765 in obtaining the repeal of the Stamp Act, they reasoned that another such congress might be able to compel a moderation of British policy and, at the same time, take the initiative away from the local radical committees. The Committee of Fifty-One therefore rejected Boston's pleas for non-intercourse, and proposed instead a general congress of delegates from all the colonies to deal with American grievances in general, and with Boston's plight in particular. The New Englanders were in no position to reject any gesture of support and, when they received a similar proposal from the Philadelphia Committee, they agreed that a congress should assemble in Philadelphia in September.[5]

The choice of Philadelphia as a meeting-place for the Congress pleased most conservatives, for, under the firm control of Galloway and the Quakers, this town had never developed into a centre of revolutionary activity. Daniel Dulany, not yet a Loyalist, but still a warm Maryland Whig, expressed his disgust at the mere, mild pity Philadelphia felt for Boston, a pity sometimes complacent and moralizing, as in the letter a Philadelphian wrote to a Boston friend, hoping that 'your town and Province will, at length, learn a little wisdom and moderation'. He went on to assure his friend that everyone in Philadelphia wanted peace, and that 'Your patriots' would get

---

[4] Becker, *Political Parties*, p. 118.
[5] Ibid.; 4 *Am. Arch.* i. 485–6; E. C. Burnett, *The Continental Congress* (New York, 1941), p. 19.

no support from Pennsylvania. 'God bless you,' he wrote in irritable benediction, 'and grant you peace and quiet.' Even John Dickinson, while promising Pennsylvania's full support, warned his Massachusetts friends of the danger to the American cause of one colony rushing ahead of the others to destruction. A similar caution was put in more pointed fashion by a Philadelphia committeeman in a letter to a New York acquaintance: 'I pity our brethren in Boston ... but some of their friends here, and I fear with you also, are too warm ... we can be of more use to our brethren when *whole* than when *broken*.' And, although the Philadelphia Committee dutifully proclaimed a day of mourning when the Boston Port Act went into effect, the Quakers, 'though tenderly sympathizing with the distressed', dissociated themselves from the public observances.[6]

When it first received Boston's request for help, the Philadelphia Committee sent back an evasive letter, saying the sentiment of the people was difficult to learn, and suggesting nothing in the way of positive help. When the radicals in the Committee proposed a non-intercourse agreement, the conservative Whigs, led by Dickinson, blocked this and carried instead a resolution calling on the Pennsylvania Assembly to unite with the assemblies of the other colonies 'in a decent but firm application to the Crown' for a redress of grievances. Then in May 1774, shortly after the Committee of Fifty-One in New York had proposed the meeting of a continental congress, Galloway, as chairman of the Pennsylvania Committee of Correspondence, made a similar proposal to the Boston Committee. He specified that the delegates should be appointed by the regular assemblies, and should meet to ascertain American rights, as well as to 'establish a political union between the two countries [Britain and the colonies], with the assent of both'. It was this proposal that the Boston Committee agreed to.[7]

While the New York conservatives apparently regarded the

---

[6] 4 *Am. Arch.* i. 332, 354, 365–6, 386, 434.
[7] Ibid. 341–2, 485–6, 556, 563; 'Letters of Thomas Wharton', *Pennsylvania Magazine of History and Biography*, xxxiii. 337.

proposed Congress mainly as a tactical expedient, the Pennsylvanians, under Galloway's tutelage, hoped that it might negotiate a permanent constitutional settlement with Britain. The old movement in support of a royal government for Pennsylvania had made the idea of constitutional change familiar there, and had also made closer relations with Britain seem a more desirable prospect than in the other colonies. In addition, the political life of Pennsylvania was perhaps less rancorous than that of New York, the intrigues less deadly, the alignments less complex. And the two outstanding political leaders of the day, Galloway and Dickinson, were both conservative and Anglophil in outlook. Unfortunately, Dickinson and Galloway were personal and political enemies. Dickinson, while long maintaining a tender regard for the American connexion with Britain, was suspicious of the schemes of formal Anglo-American union so dear to Galloway. And Galloway was narrowly determined to exclude Dickinson from any share in a settlement of the dispute with Britain.

In 1774 Galloway dominated the Pennsylvania political scene. Dickinson's influence, still great in the other colonies as a consequence of his earlier writings, had waned in Pennsylvania. Galloway, recovering from the unpopularity of his views on the Stamp Act, had been elected speaker of the Pennsylvania Assembly in 1766 and re-elected every year thereafter. He managed the Assembly through his control of the Anti-Proprietary party, and was thus able to determine the Assembly's choice of delegates to the Continental Congress, as well as draw up their instructions. Except for Galloway himself, the Pennsylvania delegates were inconspicuous men and included none of the ablest men of the Proprietary party such as Dickinson and James Wilson. Their instructions were to ascertain American rights and obtain redress for American grievances, and also to establish 'Union and harmony between Britain and America'.[8]

[8] Burnett, *Continental Congress*, p. 35; Kuntzleman, *Joseph Galloway*, pp. 98–100.

The notion of some formal, constitutional union between Britain and the colonies had long been an occasional topic of conversation in Philadelphia, but for Galloway, and almost for him alone, it had become a precise and realizable goal. Early in his career he had been interested in Anglo-American union by his mentor, Benjamin Franklin, the proponent of the Albany Plan. Franklin, however, living in England, had gradually become tired of English indifference to America, until finally he could write to Galloway: 'When I consider the extreme corruption prevalent among all orders of men in this old rotten state, and the glorious public virtue so predominant in our rising country, I cannot but apprehend more mischief than benefit from a closer union.' Such a union, Franklin concluded, would be like 'coupling and binding together the dead & the living'.[9] Galloway was unconvinced and, for him, the crisis of 1774 presented almost an ideal setting for an act of revolutionary conservatism, an act which would immortalize him as a statesman: the securing on a solid basis of an organic union among the American colonies and between them and England. Thus while Franklin thought more and more of independence and separation; while Dickinson thought still in the ancient terms of petitioning the Crown for redress of grievances; and while the New Yorkers thought mainly of finding some means of diverting New England from war, Galloway conceived of the Continental Congress as a constitutional convention; indeed, as *his* constitutional convention.

In the purposefulness of his intentions, Galloway came close to matching his New England enemies, but in his preparations for the Congress, and in his estimate of the attitudes of its members, he was woefully negligent. He made his first mistake in supposing that the delegates to the Congress would all be appointed, as were those of his own province, by the regular provincial legislatures. Here, he simply underestimated the momentum of the revolutionary movement. In all the other

[9] Benjamin Franklin, *The Complete Works of Benjamin Franklin*, ed. J. Bigelow (10 vols., New York and London, 1887–8), v. 435–9.

colonies, except Massachusetts and Rhode Island where the legislatures were already under radical control, delegates to the Congress were chosen by special conventions called for the purpose. These tended to be weighted in favour of the radicals since, in most provinces, the conservatives took little part in their formation. In Maryland delegates were chosen at a meeting 'of the Committees appointed by the several Counties'; in New Hampshire at a 'meeting of the deputies appointed by the several towns'; in North Carolina 'at a general meeting of the deputies of the Inhabitants'; and in South Carolina 'at a general meeting of the inhabitants' at Charleston, although their choice was afterwards ratified by the South Carolina Commons House of Assembly. The Virginia delegates were appointed by a 'provincial convention' summoned by a rump of the House of Burgesses.[10]

In New York the Committee of Fifty-One did manage with some difficulty to dominate the arrangements for the election of delegates to a Provincial Congress which, in turn, elected delegates to the Continental Congress. The Committee encountered unexpected trouble when the Tory districts of the province refused to take any part at all in forming a Provincial Congress, so that in these districts the radicals were able to pick their men without opposition. Colden wrote that in Orange County only twenty out of a thousand freeholders attended a meeting to elect delegates to the Provincial Congress. In Brooklyn, according to the Tories, two staunch Whigs met together, and one certified the other to be the unanimous choice of the electors as King's County delegate to the Continental Congress.[11]

Eventually, however, the Committee of Fifty-One persuaded the Provincial Congress to appoint a delegation made up of three dependable conservatives, one man without clear political

---

[10] Burnett, *Continental Congress*, pp. 20–21.

[11] Becker, *Political Parties*, pp. 127, 138–41; 4 *Am. Arch.* i. 517; *Examination of Joseph Galloway before the House of Commons in a Committee on the American Papers* (London, 1780), p. 11.

affiliations, and only one lukewarm radical. Colden wrote to Lord Dartmouth, the colonial secretary, that he thought the 'cool, prudent men' would prevail in New York, and noted that neither John Morin Scott nor Alexander McDougall, the leading radicals, were delegates to the Congress. Thomas Jones, a Tory judge, wrote that the 'friends of government' were quite satisfied with the New York delegates, and believed that they would work for a 'redress of grievances, and a firm union between Great Britain and America upon constitutional principles'.[12]

It is significant, in considering New York's preparations for the Continental Congress that, if the leading radicals of the province were not sent to Philadelphia, neither was Councillor William Smith, the man in New York closest in outlook to Galloway, and occupying in New York politics a position similar to that occupied by Galloway in Pennsylvania. Like Galloway, Smith was a political manager rather than a royal office-holder, and like Galloway he had a scheme for a permanent Anglo-American union. Unlike Galloway, Smith had vigorously opposed the Stamp Act, and along with the Livingstons and Scott had led the popular and radical opposition to Parliament in New York. As late as 1774 he seems still to have been identified with the Whigs rather than with the Tories, and it may have been this that kept him off the New York delegation to the Congress. Yet a year later, under inauspicious circumstances, Smith was to propose a plan of American union and reconciliation with Britain much the same as the plan Galloway was about to suggest to the Congress.[13] Smith's support might not have been of great help to Galloway. But that Smith was not a delegate to the Continental Congress, was not in communication with Galloway, and seems never to have realized how close he and Galloway were in their views, is

[12] 4 *Am. Arch.* i. 372, 517; Thomas Jones, *History of New York During the Revolutionary War* (2 vols., New York, 1879), i. 34–35.

[13] Becker, *Political Parties*, p. 38; *N.Y. Col. Doc.* viii. 653–4; William Smith, *Historical Memoirs*, pp. 237, 252–3; Id., *History of the Late Province of New York* (2 vols., Albany, 1829), pp. xi–xiii.

further evidence of the curious dispersion of the opponents of the Revolution.

Galloway seems not to have been alarmed at the manner in which most of the delegations to the Congress were chosen, perhaps because their instructions were so mild. Those, for example, of the Massachusetts delegates, to seek 'the recovery and establishment of their just rights and liberties . . . and the restoration of union and harmony between Great Britain and the Colonies', were similar to the judicious instructions Galloway had written for his Pennsylvania delegates, even if they did not include, as his did, a strict injunction to avoid 'everything indecent or disrespectful' to Great Britain. Altogether, five delegations were instructed to secure American rights; four were also expected to restore 'union and harmony'; two were merely to secure a redress of grievances. Only the Maryland and Virginia delegates were told specifically to consider a non-intercourse agreement.[14]

Despite the comparative uniformity of their instructions, there was real disagreement among the delegates to the Congress on measures to be pursued. Galloway afterwards wrote that as soon as the Congress met, two parties were formed, one composed of 'men of loyal principles' who wanted a peaceful settlement of the dispute with Britain, and a 'more solid and constitutional' union between them; and the other of 'congregational and presbyterian republicans' who wanted to throw off all connexion with Britain and establish American independence.[15]

The belief that most of the active revolutionists were Puritans by heritage or temperament was not Galloway's alone: it was held by almost all the Tories whose opinions survive, and its importance as a rationale of the Revolution will be discussed later. It is sufficient here to observe that Galloway's 'congregational and presbyterian republicans' were, most of them,

[14] Burnett, *Continental Congress*, chap. iii, *passim*.
[15] Joseph Galloway, *Historical and Political Reflections on the Rise and Progress of the American Rebellion* (London, 1780), p. 66.

substantial, property-owning New Englanders who neither wanted nor feared social revolution. They came to the Congress intent on getting the support of the other colonies against what they regarded as a British invasion. They were not hopeful of an easily negotiated settlement, and they regarded as fanciful and menacing any plans for a new Anglo-American constitution made while Massachusetts was burdened with an army of occupation. They had already, in 1774, come to believe that their salvation lay in affirming the independence they had always felt, though they were not yet certain that this would necessarily mean a complete political separation between Britain and America. At the Congress they were to demand a cessation of trade with England, both as a gesture of colonial unity and as a means of compelling the British mercantile community to argue the government into a moderation of its policies. Beyond this, the New Englanders seem at this time to have hoped that the Congress might become the focus of some form of American union, and that it could give central direction to a war with Britain, should this occur.

Galloway's 'men of loyal principles', on the other hand, were mostly the delegates from New York and Pennsylvania, led by Galloway himself and by James Duane and John Jay of New York. They were to be joined by a few delegates from other colonies like Stephen Hopkins of Rhode Island and John Rutledge of South Carolina. These people were not yet convinced—some of them were never to be convinced—that the British government's attitude towards America generally and towards Boston in particular was entirely without justification; and they were afraid of the social upheavals that might accompany a war with the mother country. In addition, however, their loyal principles owed a great deal to their general intellectual, social, and even physical environment. Their outlook was oligarchic, by conviction in the case of Galloway, by mere habit perhaps in the case of men like Duane and Rutledge. Their attitudes were essentially urban: hardly any of them lived more than a few minutes' walk from salt water.

As townsmen from the trading ports of New York, Philadelphia, Newport, and Charleston, they were bound by manners as well as by interest to the rest of the Atlantic community. At the Congress, with Galloway as their spokesman, they would urge a negotiated settlement with Britain, though they were willing to accept a non-intercourse agreement to conciliate the radicals and improve America's bargaining power. Beyond this, they hoped the Congress might become the nucleus of an American government, subsidiary to, and formally bound to the British government.

Unfortunately for Galloway, he seems not to have observed another distinct party at the Congress, a party with a less active programme than the others, but holding none the less a coherent point of view. This group was led by the Virginians and was made up mostly of Southerners who thought of themselves as Old Whigs. They were oligarchic in sentiment like the loyal party and, like them, were suspicious of the 'low, levelling principles' of the New Englanders. Galloway expected that the Southerners would join his group as a matter of course. There were, however, important differences in perspective between the Southern Whigs and the loyal party of the Middle Colonies. In the first place, the Southerners were agrarian rather than commercial in outlook. The South's principal products were exported, it is true, and the planters of the region were intimately involved with the merchants of Glasgow, Bristol, London, and Liverpool; but this was more often an intimacy of debt and resentment than of comradeship.

Politically, the attitude of the Southern planters was neither national or imperial, but intensely local, dominated by a fierce suspicion of any active central government. Most of the Southern leaders were already convinced that New England's quarrel with Britain was due to a wicked ministerial plot 'to overturn the constitution and introduce a system of arbitrary government'.[16] So long as they believed that the British were

---

[16] George Washington, *The Writings of George Washington*, ed. W. C. Ford (14 vols., New York, 1889–93), ii. 442.

the aggressors, and that they were fighting the classic battle of English liberty against usurping tyranny, the Southerners would support stern measures of resistance, and shun negotiation. If, however, they could be convinced that New England aimed at independence, they might support a compromise. In the summer of 1774 the only course of action of which they strongly approved was the suspension of trade with Britain, a species, after all, of the act of withdrawal by which, several times again in its history, the South was to assert its self-sufficiency, demonstrate its scorn for mere commerce, and warn of its pride.

It would not have been difficult to predict that the first Continental Congress would adopt a non-intercourse agreement, since none of the principal groups represented was opposed to commercial coercion of Britain. The real questions to be decided were whether or not the Congress would assume the powers of an American government, and whether or not any negotiations would be opened with the British government. As the most influential and eloquent leader of the conservative faction, Galloway had the task of persuading the Southern delegates that a formal constitutional settlement with Britain was the alternative, not to a war which the South did not fear, but to American independence and, with it, the prospect of an American national government less remote and less liberal than the British.

Despite his real abilities, Galloway was ill-suited to a job of conciliation and persuasion. He had, like Governor Hutchinson, the Tory oligarch's contempt for the necessities of practical politics; unlike Hutchinson, he had also a disabling vanity. Having ignored the ominous manner in which delegates to the Congress were chosen, he seems to have made no real effort during the summer of 1774 to organize support among conservatives in the other colonies. He apparently supposed he could, by mere presence and force of argument, assume the leadership of the Congress when it met. While he expected the Congress to become a constitutional convention, he seems to have expected its members to be as easily managed as those inarticulate farmers in the Pennsylvania Assembly who sat 'with their hats on, great coarse cloth coats, leather breeches, and woolen stockings in the month of July'.[17] His most serious political correspondence during these critical months was not with anyone whose support might have been valuable when the Congress met, but rather with his friend William Franklin, the royal governor of New Jersey. Whether by his design or not, his communications to Franklin were relayed to the authorities in London, and this made Galloway appear to be a sort of informer. Finally, in excluding John Dickinson from any part in the arrangements for the Congress, Galloway erred seriously, for it was Dickinson rather than Galloway himself who was at this time the natural leader of the forces of American conservatism.

In 1774 Dickinson was probably the most influential man in America. His *Farmer's Letters* had given him a reputation both in England and in the colonies as a cogent champion of American liberty. Through Charles Thomson he was in correspondence with the revolutionary leaders in New England, who trusted him while they distrusted Galloway. The Southern landowners regarded him almost as one of themselves, he being a landed proprietor without the close urban attachments which tainted Galloway and the New Yorkers. Nevertheless, Dickinson had almost a reverence for the British constitution and for English ways. He was no more convinced than Galloway of the thoroughly wicked intentions of the British government, and no less suspicious than Galloway of the separatist ambitions of Boston. It was Dickinson who, in the summer of 1774, persuaded the Pennsylvania Convention to propose a conciliatory petition to the King, rather than endorse a non-importation agreement. Moreover, Dickinson favoured sending a group of American commissioners to London to negotiate a general settlement of the disputes with Britain.[18]

[17] E. H. Baldwin, 'Joseph Galloway, the Loyalist Politician', *Pennsylvania Magazine of History and Biography*, xxvi. 296.   [18] 4 *Am. Arch.* i. 556, 563.

His moderate views did not, of course, make a Tory of Dickinson: his conservatism was traditional, aristocratic, and Whiggish; it rested on confidence and simplicity of outlook, not, as did Galloway's, on fear and calculation. Even so, his Anglophil sentiments were genuine and, had Galloway been able to work with him, perhaps to defer to him, Dickinson might have exerted a powerful moderating influence on the delegates to the Congress.

Unfortunately, the enmity between Galloway and Dickinson was too great for Galloway, at least, to overcome. In the small theatre of Pennsylvania politics the two men, though both still young, had for years jostled each other for position, beginning in 1764 when Galloway had become Franklin's lieutenant in the fight to make Pennsylvania a royal province, and Dickinson had sided with the Proprietary party. The two rivals had fought a pamphlet war, and had almost fought a duel. And now Galloway, sensing the opportunity to become an imperial statesman, was disinclined to share the stage with Dickinson. Yet, when the delegates to the Congress began to assemble in Philadelphia early in September 1774, it was Dickinson whom they sought out and consulted; it was Dickinson who entertained them, and eased away the suspicion the Virginians felt for the New Englanders. Had Galloway encouraged him, Dickinson might have become the leader of the party of negotiation; as it was, he served at a critical moment as the keystone in the arch of a war alliance between New England and the South.

Galloway was surprised and thrown off balance from the first day the Congress met by the impetus of New England organization. At their first meeting the delegates agreed to make Carpenter's Hall their regular meeting-place, and rejected Galloway's offer of the State House, 'a much more proper Place'. They then chose Charles Thomson, the radical whom some called the Sam Adams of Philadelphia, to be their secretary. Galloway wrote despairingly to Governor Franklin that both of these decisions had been 'privately settled by an Interest made out of Doors'. He was forced, he wrote sadly, to revise his earlier opinion about the moderation of the delegates; the Virginians and Carolinians, he said, 'seem much among the Bostonians'.[19]

As the Congress went into its deliberations one development after another worked to Galloway's disadvantage. The rumours of fighting near Boston stimulated a warlike spirit among the delegates, and even when proved false, left a memorable sense of New England's danger. The adoption of the inflammatory Suffolk Resolves by the Congress both weakened the conserva- tive group, and removed what small chance there might have been of the British government negotiating with the Congress. Finally, the Congress agreed to consider a non-importation agreement before discussing the plan of negotiation which Galloway had ready. In all this the New England delegates acted with remarkable circumspection, exploiting to the full the combative temper of the Southerners, while avoiding scrupulously any suggestion of constitutional innovation. 'We have been obliged to act with great delicacy and caution', John Adams wrote, '. . . to keep ourselves out of sight, . . . to insinuate our sentiments, designs and desires, by means of other persons, sometimes of one province, and sometimes of another.'[20]

While the New Englanders were keeping out of view, Gallo- way was trying to stay in view. He and his conservative as- sociates, the closest of whom was James Duane, allowed themselves, time and again, to be manœuvred into supporting what they regarded as radical measures, on the promise of being allowed to take up Galloway's plan for negotiation. Finally, after nearly a month of sessions, and after the Con- gress had unanimously adopted a non-importation agreement,

---

[19] *N.J. Archives*, 1st series, x. 475–8; Burnett, *Continental Congress*, pp. 33–34.
[20] E. C. Burnett, ed., *Letters of Members of the Continental Congress* (8 vols., Washington, 1921–36), i. 60; W. C. Ford, ed., *Journals of the Con- tinental Congress, 1774–1789* (34 vols., Washington, 1904), i. 40; Burnett, *Continental Congress*, pp. 39–46.

Galloway was permitted to introduce his plan of accommodation.[21] Here now was Galloway's first and, as it turned out, last
opportunity to exercise his imperial statesmanship in an
American forum. He made the most of his belated chance:
his argument for negotiation had logic and verve; it was persuasive and lucid, and many of the delegates who heard him
speak were to remember his cold brilliance long after the issues
he raised had been settled another way than he hoped.

Galloway began by reminding the delegates that many of
them had instructions to seek a reunion with Britain, as well
as seek the redress of grievances which had hitherto solely
occupied them. He then urged the Congress to send a deputation to England to deal directly with the government, pointing
out that, as the Congress itself would probably be regarded in
England as an illegal assembly, no mere petition would receive
any attention. To refuse to send such a deputation would, he
said, be to refuse to negotiate; to refuse to negotiate would be
to admit a desire for war and independence. What then, Galloway asked, should be the basis for negotiation? Here he found
it necessary to deal learnedly with the constitutional nature of
the troubles between the colonies and England. He defended
the logic of the British point of view, which was simply that the
British Empire was a single state, that such a state must have
a single sovereign, and that for the colonies to deny the
sovereignty of Parliament was a declaration of independence
and secession.

How, he asked, were the Americans to answer this argument
without accepting either an undesired separation from Britain,
or the intolerable burden of being governed by a power over
which they had no control? On what could American rights
be based? Galloway dismissed as self-contradictory the tor-
tuous distinctions between internal and external taxation, and
between the power of taxation and the power of general legislation. He also dismissed coldly radical arguments based on the

[21] Burnett, *Continental Congress*, p. 47; *Journals of the Continental Congress*, i. 43.

'law of Nature'. The colonies, he said, were not in a state of nature and never had been. Similarly, the 'rights of Mankind' offered no clear guidance because, as Montesquieu had shown, those rights were as various as the various forms of human government and society. No, he maintained, there was only one legitimate source of American rights, and that was the British constitution.

The essence of the English constitution as it had grown out of medieval origins was, according to Galloway, the right of representation in Parliament. He denied that the Americans were 'virtually' represented because, historically, representation was based on landownership. It was land, not people, which was represented in Parliament, and no part of the land of America had any representation whatever. In perceiving that Parliament was a territorial assembly with no rightful claim to control over lands which were not represented, Galloway went to the heart, not of the political, but of the constitutional impasse between Britain and America, and defined it clearly.[22] He concluded that, in consequence of this inherent limitation on Parliament's authority, the colonies were simply independent states: 'The law of Great Britain does not bind us in any case whatever.' By leaving the realm of England, the original colonists had lost their representation in Parliament, and unless it was 'restored' to their descendants, Parliament had no constitutional right to legislate for them.

By showing how precarious the union between Britain and America was, Galloway hoped he could shock his fellow delegates, especially the Southerners, into a willingness to salvage the British Empire from imminent dissolution. He insisted that America had no guarantees of liberty at all, natural, historical, or otherwise, except from the British constitution, and that unless they could partake directly of the

[22] L. B. Namier wrote that 'the necessary limitations to the authority of the British Parliament, a territorial assembly, were not as yet understood' at the time of the American Revolution (*England in the Age of the American Revolution* (London, 1930), p. 43). This was true in a general sense, but not for Galloway.

sacrament of representation, they would either drift into anarchy, or come under a native American government far less liberal than the British. 'Can we wish to become aliens to the mother state?' he asked; if not, 'We must come upon terms.' At heart Galloway still favoured direct American representation in Parliament, but he realized this was generally regarded, both in England and America, as impractical. He therefore proposed the plan of Anglo-American union for which he is now chiefly remembered.

The essence of Galloway's plan of union was a subsidiary American legislature with concurrent powers with Parliament over American affairs.[23] The members of this legislature, which Galloway called a 'Grand Council', would be appointed by the various provincial assemblies, and the Council would be presided over by a 'President-General' appointed by the King. Bills affecting the colonies could be introduced either in the Grand Council or in Parliament, but would have to have the assent of both to become Acts. Thus Parliament would retain the power, though no longer the exclusive power, of making general laws for the colonies, and the colonies would gain the right to participate in imperial legislation, and to disallow offensive Acts of Parliament.

Galloway ended his speech to the Congress on a philosophical and generous note. He lamented the distinction which

[23] Galloway's Plan of 1774 is different in one vital respect from Franklin's Albany Plan of 1754 (or William Penn's Plan of 1696). It provided not only for an inter-colonial union, but also for a legislative union with Britain. Galloway's Plan adopted the nomenclature of the Albany Plan, and his Grand Council, like that of the Albany Plan, would have provided for American defence, as well as controlled Indian relations and the settlement of western lands, and would have supervised inter-colonial relations in general. Galloway's Plan is printed in his pamphlet, *A Candid Examination of the Mutual Claims of Great-Britain and the Colonies* (London, 1780); in T. B. Chandler's *What Think Ye of the Congress Now?* (New York, 1775); in *N.J. Arch.*, 1st series, x. 504–7; in Adams, *Works*, ii. 387–91; and, with its later variations, in J. P. Boyd, *Anglo-American Union: Joseph Galloway's Plans to Preserve the British Empire* (Philadelphia, 1941). See also the note following the writer's article, 'The Last Hopes of the American Loyalists', *Canadian Historical Review*, xxxii. 40–42.

had grown up between Englishmen in America and at home:
'I wish to see it exploded, and the right to participate in the
supreme councils of the State extended, in some form, not only
to America, but to all the British dominions.' If this was not
done, the 'profound and excellent fabrick' of the British
Empire would be torn apart. He urged his fellow Congressmen
to put their claims to Britain freely, openly, and firmly. If they
did not like his proposal, let them suggest another. Only, 'whatever we do, let us be particular and explicit, and not wander in
general allegations', which would lead to nothing, and were
besides 'dishonourable and insidious'. If Britain refused to
come to terms, once reasonable terms were offered her, then,
Galloway said, being a friend of liberty, he would go as far as
any man in opposing her.[24]

Galloway's speech to the Congress made a favourable impression. Even John Adams admitted that he was a 'learned
and sensible' speaker. James Duane seconded his proposal, and
recalled to the delegates that the purpose of the Congress was
not merely to give immediate support to Boston, but to seek
a lasting accommodation with Britain. John Rutledge of South
Carolina said he had come to the Congress with the idea of
getting a bill of rights and a 'plan of permanent relief'. He
thought Galloway's plan could be freed from almost every
objection; he thought it was 'almost a perfect plan'.[25]

Taken out of context, or rather at face value in its apparent
context, Galloway's plea for reconciliation and union between
Britain and America is still impressive in argument and
elevated in tone. There is little hint in it of the weakness,
either of his cause or of that of his opponents, that doomed it.
It was 'almost a perfect plan', and the real objections to it are
outside its area of concern. A major objection, of course, is
inherent in Galloway's purely constitutional definition of
the quarrel between the colonies and Britain. The Congress
Galloway addressed was no constitutional convention, but an

[24] Galloway, *Historical Reflections*, pp. 70–78; *Letters of Members of the
Continental Congress*, i. 52.　　　[25] Ibid. 53–54; Adams, *Works*, ii. 396.

assembly of desperate urgency convened to deal with what, in their hearts, most of the men present felt to be a foreign invasion. In ignoring this sentiment, in ignoring the presence in Boston of an army of subjugation, Galloway exhibited an almost perverse narrowness of view. If the Congress were to be persuaded to negotiate with, rather than coerce, Britain, the first step in negotiation should of course have been to ask, decently but firmly, for the withdrawal of British troops from Boston.

On the other hand, there is something disingenuous in the reception given Galloway's proposal by the radicals in the Congress. They did not present strong arguments against the Plan; they did not amend it; they did not discuss seriously the merits of Galloway's proposal that a deputation be sent to England. The New Englanders sat wary and quiet and left the opposition to the Virginia radicals, Patrick Henry and Richard Lee, who both maintained rather speciously that Galloway's plan was revolutionary and would lead to undesirable innovations. Lee said the delegates had no power to consent to a political union with Britain. John Jay replied that they had that power as much as any other, but that, for that matter, the Plan could be submitted to the provincial assemblies for ratification. Henry maintained that Galloway's union would liberate Americans from a corrupt House of Commons only to throw them into the arms of an American legislature which the British could bribe.

After two days of inconclusive debate, and after rejecting Galloway's offer to debate the merits of his plan with one of the Virginia delegates, a motion was put to postpone consideration of the Plan to a later date, and was passed by a vote of six colonies to five. The Congress then adopted a non-exportation agreement and a resolution approving the opposition of Massachusetts to the late Acts of Parliament. Later Duane persuaded the Congress to adopt his moderate Declaration of Rights, and finally, on 20 October, the Congress unanimously adopted the Association.[26]

[26] *Letters of Members of the Continental Congress*, i. 53–59; Galloway,

In form, the Association was simply an oath promising to abide by the non-intercourse agreements. In fact, it became an oath of allegiance and loyalty to the Congress and to the local revolutionary committees, the embodiment of a transfer of sovereignty which was to turn the Tories into Loyalists, and lead the colonies into eight years of civil war. In the hope that his plan might be taken up again, Galloway and his fellow conservatives did not vote against the Association. On 22 October, however, the Congress voted to expunge all reference to Galloway's Plan from its Minutes, and then abruptly adjourned. The best chance for a negotiated settlement of the dispute with Britain had gone, and with it went twenty years of Tory hopes.[27]

Nothing in the whole history of the Revolution is more illustrative of the weakness of the Tories than that, at this most critical moment, the moment of birth of the American Union, the Tory cause should have been entrusted by default, to Joseph Galloway. For Galloway, despite what Benjamin Franklin called, 'all the usefulness of so much experience and such great abilities',[28] was fearfully inept in his brief role as leader of the scattered forces of American conservatism. He failed as a leader not merely because of the strength of the movement he opposed, and not only by a succession of tactical mistakes, but also because of his nervous and overweening anxiety to hold the centre of the political stage. With a keen mind, a remarkable store of political knowledge, uncommon energy, and a consuming ambition, he succeeded only in making the way easy for his enemies. By refusing to give leadership to the Tories, Hutchinson had failed his cause but kept his integrity. Galloway, by insisting that he alone could lead, had done great harm, both to the Tories and to himself.

A Candid Examination, pp. 70–71; Id., Historical Reflections, passim; Burnett, Continental Congress, pp. 48–55.
[27] Ibid., pp. 55–59; Letters of Members of the Continental Congress, i. 66, 67, 76.
[28] Franklin, Works, v. 87.

CHAPTER IV

The Crisis of Allegiance

THE decisions of the First Continental Congress, and the establishment of the Congress itself as the nucleus of an American national government, were mortal blows to the Tories. Never again, after October 1774, were they to control, as they had done, the main channels of government in America. Oddly enough, however, the immediate effect of this loss of place was to liberate the Tories at last from the awkward and passive role to which heretofore they had been consigned. Now finally, they had something tangible to attack: the Congress, its measures, the whole new structure of government that was being rapidly erected on a foundation of local revolutionary committees. No longer were they limited merely to apologizing for Britain and defending themselves, and soon the bitter effects of new Tory energy began to appear, first in dozens of broadsides and pamphlets, then in parades and meetings, and finally in companies of armed men loyal to the King. As may sometimes happen in war, the Tories, in being thrown strategically on the defensive, were able, indeed obliged, to go tactically on the offensive. Of course, this enlarged area of manœuvre was a poor reward for the loss of power and initiative the Tories had now suffered.

One of the first to grasp the new opportunities open to the opponents of revolution was, strange to say, Joseph Galloway. Soon after the Congress had adjourned, Galloway went to New York, as he should have done much earlier. There Duane introduced him to a number of local conservatives, among them the ancient lieutenant-governor, Cadwallader Colden. Galloway talked earnestly to Colden about his lately rejected plan of union, and Colden decided the plan was a 'rational mode of proceeding, evidently tending to a reconciliation', and he sent a copy of it to the government in London. Eventually, Lord Dartmouth wrote back a rather vague endorsement of the plan: 'The Idea of Union upon some general constitutional plan is certainly very just, & I have no doubt of its being yet attainable.'[1]

Encouraged by the hostility to the Congress of the New Yorkers whom he met, Galloway then determined to oppose publicly the measures the Congress had taken. In this he was handicapped, of course, by his own recent acquiescence in the adoption of these measures.[2] Despite having signed the Association himself, he attempted, on his return to Philadelphia, to persuade the Pennsylvania Assembly to disapprove the Proceedings of the Congress. For once, however, the Assembly would not yield to Galloway and, accepting Dickinson's advice, voted to endorse the Proceedings. Dickinson, who seems to have distrusted Galloway less than Galloway distrusted him, then pleaded with Galloway not to break with the Congress, and urged him to serve in the next one. 'His declining to serve', Dickinson said, 'would have a bad effect on the public cause.' Benjamin Franklin, still in England, also advised Galloway to support the Congress.[3] But Galloway was adamant; he retired to his home 'with a fever and colic', to write his *Candid Examination of the Mutual Claims of Great-Britain and the Colonies.*

In his *Candid Examination* Galloway attempted to draw a fine line between justifiable and unjustifiable resistance to Britain and, in so doing, to explain and rationalize his own

---

[1] *N.Y. Col. Doc.* viii. 513, 529; Becker, *Political Parties*, p. 149; Baldwin, 'Joseph Galloway', ibid., pp. 422–5; *N.J. Arch.*, 1st series, x. 38.

[2] While the Congress was still in session Galloway and Duane had adopted the curious expedient of exchanging with each other certificates affirming that they regarded as treasonable the resolution endorsing Massachusetts's opposition to Acts of Parliament. Galloway, *Examination . . . before the House of Commons*, p. 63.

[3] W. B. Reed, *Life and Correspondence of Joseph Reed* (2 vols., Philadelphia, 1847), i. 91; Franklin, *Works*, v. 435–9; Boyd, *Joseph Galloway*, pp. 38–39.

actions. Neither the advocates of unqualified resistance, he wrote, nor the advocates of unqualified submission, were 'seekers after Truth'. The colonies' grievances were genuine, and a general congress to deal with them had been warranted. The Congress, however, had failed entirely in its proper purpose, which was to seek an equitable constitutional settlement with Britain. Therefore, the colonies should individually renounce the authority of the Congress and negotiate with Britain through their legal assemblies.

Galloway was scornful of the argument he had heard at the Congress, that the colonies owed allegiance to the King, but not to Parliament. It was absurd, he wrote, to acknowledge the authority of the King, and deny the authority of the King's superior, the King-in-Parliament. He quoted Locke, that the King 'has no will, no power, but that of the law'. It was true that, 'in order to disguise their purpose of outright independence', the Congress had conceded to Parliament 'a whimsical authority', to regulate American trade. But this meant nothing so long as any colonial assembly would have the right to challenge any Act of Parliament. Who was to determine the extent of Parliament's authority? Presumably the Congress, 'an illegal motley Congress', Galloway wrote bitterly, most of its delegates chosen by a twentieth part of the people—'A blessed American constitution!'

Nevertheless, Galloway still maintained that his countrymen had a substantial complaint against Britain: they were unrepresented in Parliament. 'Most certain it is', he wrote, that this is a situation which people accustomed to liberty cannot sit easy under.' The best solution, he insisted, was his plan of union. He urged his fellow Americans to dissolve the revolutionary committees, and to pull down the arbitrary government the Congress was erecting. Then they should, 'like men who love order and government', ask for union with Britain. Concluding, Galloway ventured into the realm of dire prediction. If the present course of affairs continued, he wrote, there were three dreadful prospects before America: conquest by the British with a prolonged military occupation; independence and subsequent conquest by a foreign power; or, what Galloway thought most likely, independence and a subsequent civil war. The North and South, he thought, would quarrel over who was to dominate the West, and consequently the continent. The South, 'weak for want of discipline', and inhibited by Negro slavery, would finally be conquered and devastated by the ruthless and cunning Yankees.[4]

Dickinson and Charles Thomson wrote an answer to Galloway in which they accused him of trying to argue the Americans into 'abject slavery', and said that to acknowledge the supremacy of Parliament would leave America no rights at all. In an angry reply to his old enemy, Galloway insisted that to acknowledge Parliament's right to legislate for America did not justify any abuse of this right. 'Could the great Mr. Locke arise from the grave', he wrote, 'and hear his idea of a *'supreme power'* thus corrupted, . . . I much doubt whether all his philosophy and religion could suppress his resentment at such unintelligible jargon and horrid nonsense.' Dickinson had written that Galloway's proposed delegates would be corrupted and that the liberties of America could not be left 'to the virtues of any men, however conspicuous'. Galloway asked where the liberties of Americans could be kept safe, if not 'in the hands of their representatives, who are accountable to them?'[5]

With Galloway's disavowal of the work of the Continental Congress, his influence in Pennsylvania waned rapidly. He began, as other Tories were to do increasingly in years to come, to attach importance to what, a few months earlier, would have seemed unmentionably trivial events. By February 1775 the man who, six months before, had fully expected to write a constitution for America, was reduced to noting that 'the Tories (as they are called) make it a point to visit the Coffee House

---

[4] Galloway, *A Candid Examination*, p. 59.
[5] Id., *A Reply to an Address to the Author of a Pamphlet entitled 'A Candid Examination'* . . . etc. (London, 1775).

daily and maintain their ground'. Again, as other Tories were increasingly to do, Galloway, by now hopelessly sure of the weakness of his cause, resigned to the British the task of halting revolution. He wrote that he was certain the propertied classes would turn against the Congress, if only Britain would give them some sort of lead.[6]

Galloway's last chance to exercise any real influence, even in Pennsylvania, came when Governor John Penn asked the Pennsylvania Assembly to present its own petition of grievances to the King. Galloway managed to persuade the Assembly to consider such a petition, the adoption of which would have separated Pennsylvania from the measures pursued by the Congress. 'I censured & condemned the Measures of the Congress in every Thing', he wrote to his admiring friend Governor Franklin, '—aver'd that they all tended to incite America to Sedition & terminated [sic] in Independence—contended for & proved the Necessity of Parliamentary Jurisdiction over the Colonies. . . . I stood single & unsupported, among a Set of Men every one of whom had approved of the Measures I was censuring.' Fourteen of the thirty-eight members of the House, Galloway wrote, came over to his side. He was unable to win a majority, however, and the radicals finally persuaded the Assembly to refer the question of a petition to the Philadelphia 'Committee of Independents'. His enemies claimed justifiably that they had 'flung Galloway'. Dispirited and frightened for his safety (during the debates he had been threatened, and a halter had been left at his door), Galloway left the Assembly and retired to 'Trevose', his farm in Bucks County.[7]

Shortly after his return from England, Galloway's old preceptor, Benjamin Franklin, visited him at 'Trevose'. Galloway urged Franklin to promote a reconciliation between the colonies and England. In reply, Franklin read Galloway most

[6] *N.J. Arch.*, 1st series, x. 573; 'Some Letters of Joseph Galloway, 1774–1775', *Pennsylvania Magazine of History and Biography*, xxi. 480–1.

[7] *N.J. Arch.*, 1st series, x. 573–4, 585–7; Kuntzleman, *Joseph Galloway*, pp. 129–32; Galloway, *Examination . . . before the House of Commons*, p. 54.

of the journal, filled with accounts of English apathy and truculence, that he had kept in England. He told Galloway that he had despaired of the British offering anything America could accept, and begged him to return to the Congress. Galloway refused, and saw no more of Franklin. The Second Congress granted Galloway's request that he be dismissed; a Connecticut delegate wrote that he was 'justly despised and Contemned by all'.[8]

So ended the more respectable part of the public career of Joseph Galloway. Now the man who had saved himself many a political hurdle by attaching himself to Benjamin Franklin, and who had married the only available lady in Pennsylvania whose father owned a four-wheeled carriage, was on his own at last. He was to retain his energies and ambitions, but never to regain his influence. Perhaps the best thing that may be said of Galloway is that he remained unswervingly committed to his own union with Britain. He did not, like many of his friends, pay with his principles for personal ease and security. Since, however, he was really to suffer for his principles, it is a pity that Galloway had not kept them quite unstained. It is a pity that he was pompous, conspiratorial, petty, and vain.

The direct attack upon the revolutionary structure of government begun by Galloway soon was taken up by a number of Tory writers. The most effective of these was a group of Anglican clerics in New York, but, surprisingly, there was one last flicker of protest from the remnants of the Tory establishment in Boston. It is ironic that Boston, regarded by all good Tories as the very centre of rebellion and fanaticism in the colonies, was the only town, except for New York, where there was a Tory press and where printers would accept Tory pamphlets. In the letters of *Massachusettensis*, written by Daniel Leonard,

---

[8] Ibid., p. 55; Hutchinson, *Diary*, ii. 237; Kuntzleman, *Joseph Galloway*, p. 137; *Letters of Members of the Continental Congress*, i. 93; Benjamin Franklin, *Autobiographical Writings*, ed. C. Van Doren (New York, 1945), p. 403.

and in the answering letters of *Novanglus*, written by John Adams, the Tory and revolutionist points of view, respectively, were presented with singular calm and care. Both Adams and Leonard wrote fairly and astutely, although neither avoided entirely the temptations of partisanship. The series was published in the *Massachusetts Gazette* during the winter of 1774-5, and it is a credit to Boston's composure that Adams and Leonard were able to debate the philosophical issues and constitutional niceties of the dispute with Britain at a time when open war between the British troops and the militia was expected hourly.

Leonard's Toryism was uncompromising and vigorous. He wrote that Massachusetts was in a state of outright rebellion, and would probably be deserted by the other colonies and conquered by the British. He likened the 'unaccountable frenzy' that had brought this about to Boston's earlier delusions about witches. A naturally excitable and credulous people, he thought, had been led to believe by 'perpetual incantation' that the British were engaged in an elaborate and devilish plot against them. Yet the only real conspirators were the revolutionists themselves, who intended to establish a local oligarchy ('not even a democracy') unembarrassed by interference from Britain, or by British concepts of liberty and justice.

Leonard put forth in skilful detail the usual Tory arguments for Parliament's supremacy, and denounced the Congress for having assumed legislative authority over the colonies, instead of seeking a settlement with Britain. He damned the new tyranny of the committees of inspection, 'where the same persons are at once legislators, accusers, witnesses, judges and jurors, and the mob the executioners'. It was astonishing, he wrote, that men allegedly in pursuit of liberty should allow arbitrary power, 'in such a hideous form and squalid hue', to get a footing among them. Leonard's conclusions were philosophical: When government is destroyed, whether by men who love liberty or by men who do not, there are then no laws to protect the weak against the powerful, or the good against the wicked: 'This is what is called a state of nature. I once thought it chimerical.'[9]

According to John Adams, the *Letters of Massachusettensis* made 'a very visible impression on many minds', which Adams, as *Novanglus*, did his best to offset. He protested the innocence of the revolutionists of plotting against the Crown as Leonard had charged. He pointed out that the Whigs had never conducted intrigues 'at a distant court' as the Tories had done, but had made their appeal only to the people, whom they could then hardly be charged with enslaving. Adams maintained the Whigs had acted on the defensive from first to last, in the old English tradition of resisting tyranny, and would gain from their resistance to Parliament, just as the English had gained by resistance to Charles I and James II. The reason England could not respect this resistance was that the people of England had become 'depraved' and Parliament 'venal'. Adams dismissed Leonard's fears of a new tyranny as alarmist, and dwelt with pleasure on the unity of the American spirit which the committees had discovered and given voice to: 'one understanding, . . . one great, wise, active and noble spirit, one masterly soul, animating one vigorous body'.[10]

In his last letter Leonard warned of the irresistible power which Britain could, if roused, bring to bear against her colonies: 'Can any of you that think soberly upon the matter, be so deluded as to believe that Great Britain, who so lately carried her arms with success to every part of the globe, triumphed over the united powers of France and Spain, and whose fleets give law to the ocean, is unable to conquer us?'[11] This theme of Britain's awful power was shortly taken up, in the columns of the *Gazette*, by another Boston Tory, Jonathan Sewell, the attorney-general of Massachusetts. After numbering the advantages to America of being part of the British

---

[9] John Adams and Daniel Leonard, *Novanglus and Massachusettensis* (Boston, 1819), pp. 142–3, 150, 158, 166, 188.
[10] Ibid., pp. 10, 14, 28, 43.   [11] Ibid., p. 5.

Empire, Sewell described in imaginative detail the suffering which a war for independence would cause. He chided the Whigs for their 'childish petulance' in asking more from Britain than Britain could honourably give: 'Think how vain it is for *Jack, Sam,* or *Will,* to war against Great Britain, now she is in earnest!'[12] Just after the publication of Sewell's almost good-humoured admonitions, the battles of Lexington and Concord brought to a close the period of free discussion in New England.

When John Adams went through New York in August 1774 on his way to the meeting of the Continental Congress, Philip Livingston told him that a number of Anglican clergymen, in particular Thomas Chandler and Myles Cooper, were engaged day and night in writing letters and sending dispatches to the other colonies and to England. Livingston thought they were trying to form 'an union of the Episcopal party, through the continent, in support of ministerial measures'.[13] Actually, Cooper thought he had already brought such a union into being.

For years, a number of Anglican clergymen, including almost all the missionaries of the Society for the Propagation of the Gospel, had waited patiently, but in growing bewilderment, for the politicians, or the royal officials, or the British government itself, to halt the advance of sedition and rebellion. Finally, a number of the more vigorous and contentious of these men had decided to act on their own responsibility. In 1773, after the Boston Tea Party, Cooper had sought out Jonathan Boucher in his Maryland parish. Some of the Virginia clergy had already asked Boucher to work out some way of forming a 'general and uniform line of conduct' for the Episcopal clergy in America. Cooper had such a plan in mind

[12] 4 *Am. Arch.* i. 1184–8; ii. 100–3, 286–9, 325. In the early 1770's Sewell had been the principal advocate in the New England press of the Tory point of view. Until late in life John Adams, who had been Sewell's best friend, believed that he, rather than Leonard, had written the *Letters of Massachusettensis.* Adams, *Works,* iv. 10.

[13] Becker, *Political Parties,* p. 158; Adams, *Works,* ii. 348.

himself, and persuaded Boucher to go with him to Philadelphia where the two men discussed an Anglican political programme with Provost William Smith.

Although Smith was still on good terms with the Presbyterians in Philadelphia, he seemed to agree with Cooper and Boucher on the necessity of opposing the fomenters of rebellion. According to Boucher, a 'plan for joint action, . . . was thereupon formed and agreed to', Cooper acting on behalf of the Northern clergy, Smith for the Pennsylvanians, and Boucher for the Maryland and Virginia clergy. When it came to agreeing on the details of a political campaign, however, Smith was evasive, as he had been at the time of the Bishop's Controversy, and the Anglicans were therefore not able to take a public stand on the question of relief for Boston, or the calling of the Continental Congress.

To the disgust of Cooper and Boucher, Smith and the rest of the Philadelphia clergy finally refused to consider any joint measures. Several of the Philadelphians joined the Whigs, and did all they could to put the Continental Congress spiritually at ease.[14] The Southerners, except for Boucher, were either apathetic or were intimidated into silence, and the burden of conducting an Anglican opposition to the Revolution thus fell to the New Yorkers. They duly made a brave agreement among themselves to 'watch and confute all publications that threatened mischief to the Church of England and the British government in America'.[15]

Although Myles Cooper had taken the lead in organizing the Anglicans for political warfare, and although he had written extensively against the Whigs in earlier years, he did not now prove to be the strongest of the Anglican controversialists. Perhaps his temperament was too convivial for times grown so rancorous. He shortly returned to his native England

[14] Jonathan Boucher, *Reminiscences of an American Loyalist*, ed. J. Bouchier [sic] (Boston, 1925), pp. 100–1.

[15] E. E. Beardsley, *Life and Correspondence of the Rt. Rev. Samuel Seabury, D.D.* (Boston, 1881), p. 30.

where, during the years of the Revolution, he was to dine well, drink liquors 'of a most delicate Texture', and then die one day at lunch. The ablest of the Anglican writers in New York were Charles Inglis, Samuel Seabury, and Thomas Chandler. Between the autumn of 1775 and the spring of 1776, with the assistance of James Rivington's press,[16] they were to put the Tory case against the Revolution with considerable skill and increasing vehemence.

Charles Inglis, the senior curate at Trinity Church, was an Ulsterman and a S.P.G. missionary. Except for Jonathan Boucher, he was perhaps the most profound of the Tory writers in the period of the Revolution. Only he and Boucher were able to raise the Tory argument, for more than a moment, from the level of politics to the higher ground of philosophy, there to discover between themselves and the revolutionists an unbridgeable chasm. Inglis's most important work was written in the form of a reply to Tom Paine's *Common Sense*, and it, along with Boucher's writings, will be discussed later. Inglis opened the Anglican attack on the Revolution with a series of letters signed 'A New York Farmer', which were published in the New York *Gazette*, and in which he dwelt chiefly on the calamities of civil war.[17]

More significant at the time than Inglis's letters, were the little Tory pamphlets called *The Letters of a Westchester Farmer*. They were written by Samuel Seabury and published by Rivington between November 1774 and January 1775. Sea-

[16] By 1774 New York was the only town in the colonies except Boston, and by 1775 the only town, where the press was open to the Tories as well as the Whigs. James Rivington, an English printer who had come to New York a few years earlier, printed most of the New York Tory writings, as well as writings by Galloway and other Tories outside New York who could not find printers in their own provinces. In addition to printing pamphlets, Rivington opened the columns of his New York *Gazetteer* to the Tories, although he also, at first, printed Whig articles. Hugh Gaine, a Belfast Episcopalian, printed both Tory and Whig articles in his New York *Gazette and Weekly Mercury*. Both Gaine and Rivington eventually became Loyalists, and Rivington's *Gazetteer*, after a brief interruption, resumed publication as the *Royal Gazette* during the British occupation of New York.

[17] Lydekker, *Life of Inglis*, pp. 145–6.

the letters of a Westchester Farmer

bury was perhaps the best propagandist, except for Tom Paine, that the Revolution produced on either side. Like Chandler, he was a New Englander by birth, and a Yale man; and like Chandler's, Seabury's Toryism and his dislike of New England Puritanism had something of the fervour of apostasy. Seabury's father had been drawn into the Anglican ministry by the anti-Puritan heresy which had for a time led Yale away from the paths of orthodoxy. Seabury himself had been brought up an Episcopalian during the exciting days of the Great Awakening, and had once watched the 'ignorant and fanatical' followers of some itinerant revivalist burn Church of England vestments and books in the streets of New London, Connecticut.

In keeping with the sensible practice of so many colonial clergymen, Seabury had studied medicine (in Edinburgh) after he finished his readings in theology. He then returned to his native land as a missionary of the Society for the Propagation of the Gospel, going first to New Jersey, then to Long Island, and finally to Westchester County, New York. Seabury was a popular preacher, his church described as 'always crowded & often so that all have not room to Sit'. He had worked faithfully, first to arrest the decline of religion and the spread of deism, and then to discourage the fanaticism which the 'daily succession of strolling preachers' who followed in George Whitefield's steps aroused. Seabury wrote that his 'love of order' made him dislike equally 'every degree of scepticism and enthusiasm', and his hostility to the Revolution was the more intense, as the Revolution seemed to him to fuse together in horrid alliance these contrary evils.[18]

Seabury had taken an active part in the Bishop's Controversy, and as early as 1770 had preached against the 'clamourers for liberty', and had written Tory articles. Most of the arguments he now used in his *Letters* reflected the increasing heat of social conflict, being free from philosophical refinement and, in the earlier letters, free from serious political or constitutional

[18] Seabury, *Letters of a Westchester Farmer*, pp. 1–20; Beardsley, *Life of Seabury*, pp. 1–29.

Seabury – Soc. for the Propagation
of the Gospel.

discussion. Seabury appealed frankly to the prejudices of his readers, particularly their rural prejudices. In his first pamphlet he described in convincing detail how the Non-Importation Agreement would punish the farmers to the advantage of profiteering merchants. He beguiled his readers with little fables about how 'Tim Twistwell, a Rascal from New-England' would take advantage of the confused times to prey on honest New Yorkers, who would have no redress because the courts would be shut down.

If committees of inspection were chosen as the Congress had recommended, Seabury warned, they would have the right to come into people's houses to see whether they drank tea or wore English woollens, 'to examine your tea-cannisters and molasses-jugs, and your wives and daughters petty-coats'. Offenders could be publicly denounced as 'enemies of American Liberty' and be outlawed by the simple fiat of 'their High-Mightinesses', the committeemen. 'O rare American Freedom!' Seabury wrote: 'Will you choose such Committees? Will you submit to them, should they be chosen by the weak, foolish, turbulent part of the country people?—Do as you please: but, by HIM that made me, I will not.—No, if I must be enslaved, let it be by a KING at least, and not by a parcel of upstart lawless Committee-men. If I must be devoured, let me be devoured by the jaws of a lion, and not *gnawed* to death by rats and vermin.' Should any committeeman come to *his* house and give himself airs, Seabury wrote, 'a good hiccory cudgel shall teach him better manners'. He concluded by urging his readers to 'behave like Englishmen', and renounce committees and congresses altogether.[19]

In *The Congress Canvassed* Seabury made a more serious indictment of the Congress, and also of New England's ambitions. He observed that Massachusetts had already asserted its complete independence, the rebels having taken control of the militia, closed the courts, dissolved the old government, and begun to set up a new one. These acts, he thought, were not in

---

[19] Seabury, *Letters of a Westchester Farmer*, pp. 46–68.

response to a sudden emergency, but were the result of a premeditated desire for independence. The New Englanders had deliberately provoked a crisis in which the other colonies would support them, believing 'that God had made Boston for himself, and all the rest of the world for Boston'.

As for the Congress, Seabury wrote that it had been an illegal body from the beginning, since neither the self-constituted provincial conventions, nor the colonial assemblies themselves, had any right to endow the Congress with the powers it had assumed. Instead of forming 'some reasonable and probable scheme' for settling the dispute with Britain, the Congress had set itself up as an American government. Seabury observed that the Association was really a legislative act, and that the use of terms such as 'recommend' and 'voluntary' meant little when the committees were to compel popular compliance, if necessary, by the use of force. His strongest criticism Seabury reserved for those who excused all such extreme measures by pleading 'the necessity of the times'. It was morally wrong, he wrote (presumably laying down his 'hiccory cudgel'), to condone acts of violence and coercion until all legal and moderate measures had been tried.[20]

Alexander Hamilton, then a precocious student at King's College, wrote a reply[21] to the *Westchester Farmer*, in which he maintained that the real issue was simply 'whether the inhabitants of Great Britain have a right to dispose of the lives and properties of the inhabitants of America or not'. He stayed close to the question of taxation, and dismissed Seabury as 'presumptuous' for having questioned the 'equity, wisdom and authority' of the Congress. In his reply to Hamilton,[22] Seabury admitted that, since the Whigs had the presumption to question the authority of King and Parliament, he had presumed to question the less well-established authority of the

[20] Ibid., pp. 69–99.
[21] Alexander Hamilton, *A Full Vindication of the Measures of the Congress* (New York, 1774).
[22] Seabury, *Letters of a Westchester Farmer*, pp. 101–48.

Congress. Here, though perhaps he did not quite realize it, Seabury was skirting the fundamental problem of allegiance that was about to divide the stream of American life into two currents.

Hamilton had written rather grandly of the 'natural' rights of mankind. Seabury replied that in a state of nature men would be free of all the restraints of law, and would thus be in a jungle where the strong would oppress the weak indiscriminately. 'I think', he observed drily, 'the form of government we lately enjoyed a much more eligible state to live in.' He agreed, he wrote, that liberty was a good thing, and slavery a very bad thing. But he preferred the liberty he had always enjoyed under King and Parliament to the more abundant liberty promised him by the agents of armed mobs.

Although the Whig argument that 'if we are taxed a penny we may be taxed a pound', was foolish, it was true, Seabury admitted, that America ought to have a fixed constitution, and not be governed in the same 'lax and precarious' manner as formerly. He did not suggest a legislative union with Britain, as Galloway had done. Rather he thought all would be well if the assemblies were left to raise internal revenue, while Parliament provided for general defence by levying duties on American trade. He appealed in his last letter to the New York Assembly to renounce the Congress, and then petition the King and Parliament for a 'solid American constitution'. 'If the people of New England will kindle a fire', he wrote, 'and then rush into it, have we no way to shew our regard and affection for them, but to jump in after them? Let us rather keep out, that we may have it in our power to pull them out, before they are burnt to death.'[23]

Where Seabury was caustic and pugnacious, Thomas Chandler was bitter and gloomy. Chandler lacked Seabury's humour and his style, but as the most partisan of Tory writers he was even better suited to the rising temper of the times. The two

---

[23] Seabury, *Letters of a Westchester Farmer*, pp. 153–62.

Chandler

pamphlets[24] which Chandler published at about the same time as Seabury's pamphlets appeared were didactic and moralizing in tone, suggesting Chandler's profession, and perhaps also his New England origins. Chandler, however, exulted in an almost malevolent dislike of New England, and warned the people of the other provinces that the New Englanders were not mere, sensible Englishmen like themselves, fighting for old English liberties, but rather, under their sober, Puritan demeanour, were 'hair-brained fanaticks' as mad as the Anabaptists of Münster.

All 'gross and enormous . . . wickedness', Chandler wrote sententiously, was achieved gradually, and all rebellions proceeded from step to step, their leaders denying at each stage that anything more was contemplated. Just as, at the beginning of the Grand Rebellion, no one intended to kill the King, so now no one openly advocated an independent American republic. Nevertheless, this was what would result from the course the Congress was following, and it would mean the eventual domination of America by the republican zealots of Boston. Chandler warned that the Anglicans, Quakers, Baptists, and Lutherans, as well as the 'moderate and candid' part of the Presbyterians, would find themselves brought under a stern Puritan yoke, if not in religion, then in politics and manners. The Germans and Dutch and other foreigners who had prospered from the mildness of British ways would suffer from the xenophobia of the New Englanders, and would be subject to a double portion of 'rancour and severity'.

Chandler was at least emphatic in his disapproval of the Continental Congress: 'Its first appearance', he wrote, 'raised our curiosity, but excited no terror. But it was not long, before it turned out to be a perfect monster,—a *mad, blind* monster!' Its delegates had utterly disregarded their instructions to seek a reunion with Britain, and had instead assumed the powers of government themselves. The New England 'master builders',

[24] *A Friendly Warning to All Reasonable Americans* (New York, 1774) and *What Think Ye of the Congress Now?* (New York, 1775).

Chandler

Chandler went on, aided by thoughtless Southern gentlemen, were now using the Congress as a means of establishing their republic, and the New Yorkers were receiving as little consideration from an actual representation in the Congress as they had from a 'virtual' representation in Parliament. Instead of denying absolutely the legitimacy of the Congress, as Seabury had done, Chandler admitted the existence of an *'Original Contract'* between the Congress and the people of the colonies. But since the Congress had not done the work it had been authorized to do, and had usurped powers never given it, the contract was dissolved, and the people owed the Congress no obedience or respect. Carrying out his theory of a social contract, Chandler maintained that if the Congress could dissolve America's contract with Parliament, the New York Assembly might dissolve New York's contract with the Congress.

As Seabury had done, Chandler ended his denunciation of the Congress with an impassioned plea that New York declare its independence of America and open its own negotiations with Britain. He urged the Assembly not to sanction the Proceedings of the Congress and act as the 'rear guard of rebellion'. Ever since the conquest of Canada, he wrote, Americans had been bloated with a vain opinion of their power and importance and blinded by an arrogant conviction of their own rightness. Let New Yorkers at least accept the possibility that they might have a doubtful cause, and let them come to terms with Britain: 'Are you afraid', he asked, '. . . of appearing singular in doing what is right?'[25]

The writings of Seabury and Chandler were widely read and well received in the Middle Colonies, especially in New York, where they added to the difficulties of the conservative Whigs who were still trying to keep control of the local radicals by supporting the Congress. Colden wrote to Lord Dartmouth that

[25] Chandler did not share Seabury's view that British taxation was unobjectionable: 'It is time', he wrote, 'that we were exempted, in a regular way, from parliamentary taxation, on some generous and equitable plan.' He thought, however, that if the colonies offered to contribute fairly to the cost of imperial defence, they would be exempted from taxation by Parliament.

the merchants in New York were opposed to non-importation, and that the great majority of the province disapproved of the Congress and were fearful of civil war. But the New York City conservatives, Colden wrote, insisted that they had to support the measures of the Congress in order to protect the city from the mob, 'that if they did not, the most dangerous men among us would take the lead'.[26]

Outside the town of New York, however, the conservative and anti-New-England feelings of the people began to find open expression. Led often by Episcopal clergymen, of whom the most active was Seabury, one town after another refused to choose committees of inspection as recommended by the Congress. When, for example, the Whig freeholders of Oyster Bay gathered to choose a committee, 'there appeared such a number of friends to our happy regular established Government, under the Crown and Parliament of *Great Britain*', that the meeting was declared illegal and adjourned. In King's District, Albany County, a public meeting of freeholders resolved to preserve the established local government against all 'daring insults to government'. A majority of the freeholders of the town of Jamaica signed a Loyalist oath, and in Dutchess County a majority of freeholders signed an oath in which they swore to defend each other against attack by any 'riotous or illegal' bodies, and to obey the laws of the land, notwithstanding the Continental Congress. They also agreed to 'promote, encourage, and when called upon, enforce' obedience to the rightful authority of King and Parliament. In Ulster County a Loyalty Pole was set up, and inscribed with a Tory oath, while in Poughkeepsie a Liberty Pole which the Whigs had set up was declared a 'publick nuisance' and was cut down by a constable and the sheriff.[27]

Noting increased signs of disaffection to the Congress,

[26] 4 *Am. Arch.* i. 957; Cadwallader Colden, 'The Colden Letter Books, 1760–1775', New York Historical Society, *Collections*, x (New York, 1887), 372.

[27] 4 *Am. Arch.* i. 1063, 1076–7, 1164, 1192, 1230; ii. 176; A. C. Flick, *Loyalism in New York During the American Revolution* (New York, 1901), pp. 37–57.

Colden, then the acting governor of New York, decided to risk having the Assembly meet. He wrote to Dartmouth that, should the Assembly prove not to be conciliatory, he could prorogue it. When it did meet in January 1775, a motion was promptly made that the House should endorse the Proceedings of the Continental Congress. This motion was warmly supported by the moderate Whigs from New York City, who maintained that the Congress itself could most effectively negotiate with Britain, and that it would do grave harm to the whole American cause if one province should follow a separate course from the others. More cannily, they dwelt on the danger of leaving resistance to Britain in radical hands, and argued that the best chance of preventing violent measures lay in the conservatives staying with the Congress.

The Tories replied that the Congress had already adopted violent measures, that it was an unconstitutional body, and that it would be far better to desert the other colonies than to desert Britain. The motion to approve the Proceedings of the Congress was thereupon defeated by one vote. The Whigs lost all chance of reversing the vote when two more Tories arrived from remote counties, and one Whig went over to the Tories.[28]

The Assembly then refused to appoint a delegation to the Second Continental Congress and instead drew up its own petition of grievances to send to England. Separate petitions were sent to the King, the Lords, and the Commons. The petition to the House of Commons acknowledged Parliament's 'supreme direction and government' over the whole Empire, but protested against the taxation of the colonies for revenue. The petition to the King acknowledged his sovereignty, expressed gratitude for his protection, and stated that 'several of the measures pursued by the colonies are by no means justifiable'. It also declared that Americans ought to have all the liberties of Englishmen and while agreeing that New York should contribute to the cost of imperial defence asked that the As-

[28] 4 *Am. Arch.* i. 1189, 1286–7, 1291–3.

sembly should be allowed to raise whatever contribution was agreed on.[29]

The action of the New York Assembly was bitterly condemned by the radicals, although even Alexander MacDougall admitted that the Assembly had followed the sentiments of the province.[30] To the Tories in the other colonies, the separatism of the Assembly, along with the writings of Seabury and Chandler, made New York seem a sort of promised land. A Philadelphia man wrote to a New York friend that 'Your assembly is revered by all sensible men in this City for . . . first making a stand.' A gentleman in Baltimore wrote to a New Yorker that 'The friends here to true liberty, are charmed with the late conduct of your respectable Council and Assembly.' Another Marylander praised the Assembly and wrote that Chandler's *What Think Ye of the Congress Now?* had brought many waverers back to loyalty. A man in Kent County, Delaware, wrote that Chandler's *Friendly Address* had done great good there, and that people were beginning to whisper their dislike of the Congress's proceedings.[31]

Galloway wrote to a New York acquaintance that Chandler's and Seabury's pamphlets had 'produced a happy effect' in Pennsylvania. He wished more copies were available. Still, he thought, they all had 'capital Defects' because 'they do not own that we have any Grievance and consequently nothing is pointed out as a Constitutional Remedy'. He thought the 'inquisitive Reader' would be dissatisfied, and that people would continue to follow the Congress unless some other course was proposed which took into account the real objections of America to arbitrary government.[32]

A good many radicals were worried about the influence New York's action might have on the other colonies. If the other Middle Colonies should negotiate separately with Britain, the whole work of the Congress might be undone, and Boston

---

[29] Ibid. 1313–21.   [30] Becker, *Political Parties*, p. 177.
[31] 4 *Am. Arch.* i. 1180, 1190, 1194, 1230–1.
[32] 'Some Letters of Joseph Galloway', ibid., pp. 480–1.

left isolated. This possibility was forestalled, however, by the outbreak of fighting in New England in the spring of 1775, an occurrence made possible by British thoughtlessness in sending an army to Boston unaccompanied by a policy.

CHAPTER V

The Tory Rank and File

In the folk tales of nineteenth-century America, two kinds of Loyalists were remembered, presumably because a certain romantic interest clung to them. There were the Tory gentlefolk, Royalists who lived in great houses and drove about in fine carriages; and there were fearful outlaws who, in these remembrances, generally travelled with Indians—'Tories and Indians'. With the disappearance of the frontier and the Indians, the outlaw Tories were forgotten, and historians, in attempting to rationalize the legends of a Tory gentry, slipped into an easy explanation of the Revolution in class terms. By this account, the Tories were either frightened or selfish oligarchs, who had fought the Revolution in order to protect their special privileges. Although traces of this view still survive, more recent students have emphasized the dangers of making class generalizations about the Revolution.

Certainly there are a woeful number of exceptions to any generalizations that may be made about the Loyalists. Besides, at first glance, there seems little useful that might be said in the same breath about Governor Hutchinson, say, and a Carolina backwoodsman; or about William Byrd of Westover, and a Brooklyn shopkeeper. Yet if the Tories are to be really understood, and if their dissent from a major decision of their countrymen is to be at all meaningful, an attempt must be made to see them in social rather than in merely individual terms. And it may be that in the very diversity of the Tory ranks there can be found a clue to the identity of the 'army'.

Of all the approaches that might be used in an attempt to separate intelligibly the Loyalists from their Patriot kinsmen, that of occupation or social class seems the least fruitful. There was indeed a Tory oligarchy, but there was also a Whig oligarchy, and if in New England the Tory proportion of ruling families was greater than the Tory proportion of the total population, in the Southern Colonies the reverse was true. Even in New England the Loyalists were hardly the gentry pictured in legend. When an Act of Banishment was passed against some three hundred Loyalists in Massachusetts in 1778, they were listed by trade or profession. About a third were merchants, professional men, and gentlemen; another third were farmers, and the rest were artisans or labourers with a sprinkling of small shopkeepers.[1]

Most random lists of Loyalists show even less evidence of gentility than this. Always the gentlemen, esquires, merchants, and the like are far outnumbered by the yeomen, cordwainers, tailors, labourers, masons, blacksmiths, and their fellows.[2] The social heterogeneity of the New York Tories is evident in the list of people arrested there in June 1776 on suspicion of plotting to assassinate General Washington. These people included the mayor of New York, some other officials and gentlemen, some farmers, several tavern-keepers, a shoemaker, two doctors, several apprentices and labourers, two tanners, a silversmith, a saddler, two gunsmiths, a tallow chandler, a miller, a schoolmaster, a former schoolmaster, a former constable, a 'pensioner with one arm', and one unfortunate man described only as 'a damned rascal'.[3]

Clearly, none of the simpler economic determinants was at

[1] The following occupations were mentioned in the Massachusetts Act of Banishment: farmer, gentleman, merchant, official, mariner, yeoman, trader, physician, labourer, clerk, blacksmith, printer, shopkeeper, bookkeeper, distiller, barrister, tidewaiter, cabinetmaker, tailor, carter, founder, carpenter, wharfinger, housewright, miller, baker, bookbinder, tallow chandler, saddler, peruke-maker, boatman, and cordwainer. See E. A. Jones, *The Loyalists of Massachusetts* (London, 1930).

[2] See, for example, the occupations listed in the appendix of E. C. Wright, *The Loyalists of New Brunswick* (Ottawa, 1955). An excellent account of Tory heterogeneity may be found in E. B. Greene, *The Revolutionary Generation, 1763–1790* (New York, 1943), chap. ix.

[3] 4 *Am. Arch.* vi. 1157–8.

work separating Whigs from Tories. Economic influences, however, may account in part for the pattern of geographical distribution that appears when the Loyalist strongholds are considered. The main centres of Tory strength fall into two distinct regions: The first was along the thinly settled western frontier, from Georgia and District Ninety-Six in South Carolina, through the Regulator country of North Carolina and the mountain settlements of Virginia, Pennsylvania, and New York, to the newly-occupied Vermont lands. The other was the maritime region of the Middle Colonies, including western Long Island and the counties of the lower Hudson Valley, southern New Jersey, the three old counties of Pennsylvania around Philadelphia, and the peninsula between Delaware and Chesapeake Bays. There were also locally important concentrations of Tories elsewhere along the Atlantic seaboard: at Charleston, around Wilmington and Norfolk, and around Newport and Portsmouth in New England.

In the West and in the tidal region of the Middle Colonies Loyalists and neutrals may have formed a majority of the population. In the areas of dense agricultural settlement, however, including the plantation country of the Southern Colonies, the thickly settled parts of the Piedmont, and most of New England, Loyalists were comparatively scarce. All that the Tory regions, the mountain and maritime frontiers, had in common was that both suffered or were threatened with economic and political subjugation by richer adjoining areas. The geographical concentration of the Tories was in peripheral areas, regions already in decline, or not yet risen to importance.

It is not difficult to explain the Loyalism of the West. The Appalachian frontiersmen—hunters, trappers, and fur traders —feared the advance of close settlement which would destroy their economy. Like the Indians of the region, many of the frontiersmen were loyal to Britain because the British government was the only force they could rely on to check the rapid advance of agricultural settlement. The tidal region of the Middle Colonies, on the other hand, still had political power, but was in danger of losing it to the more populous districts inland. Moreover, this region formed part of an Atlantic community. It looked eastward; its ties with Britain were closer than its ties with the new West. Even in New England the truly maritime regions seem to have been less than enthusiastic in their support of the Revolution. Newport lacked zeal; Nantucket and Martha's Vineyard were opportunist or neutral, and the Maine coast grew steadily less faithful to the Revolution, until Nova Scotia's Loyalism of necessity was reached.[4]

Whether the St. Lawrence Valley should be considered a separate province, or whether it merely combined the characteristics of a thinly settled and a maritime region, it too was indifferent or hostile to the Revolution. Undoubtedly some of Vermont's capriciousness during the period may be ascribed to the pull of the St. Lawrence. In any case, wherever regions newly or thinly settled touched the sea, there the Revolution was weakest: in Quebec, in Nova Scotia, in Georgia, and in New York where the Hudson carried the Atlantic world into the mountains. Wherever sailors and fishermen, trappers and traders outnumbered farmers and planters, there Tories outnumbered Whigs.

Of course a major insufficiency of such a geographical analysis is that it takes no account of important cultural influences, differences in nationality and religion mainly, that played a great role in the Revolution. The Canadians of the St. Lawrence Valley were suspicious of the Revolution, not only because they lived far outside its physical homeland, but also because they were French and Catholic, and the Revolution seemed to them English and Protestant. No geographic or economic considerations can explain the Tory villages on Long Island, intermingled with Whig villages. The Tory villages were Dutch, while the others had been settled by New Englanders. Here again, legend has done a disservice to students of the Revolution. The Loyalists were seldom more English

[4] See J. B. Brebner, *The Neutral Yankees of Nova Scotia* (New York, 1937).

than the patriots. There were, of course, many British-born Tories whose allegiance to England was habitual and natural. But, apart from these, the Tories more commonly drew their recruits from the non-English than from the English parts of the community. The two most purely English provinces, Virginia and Massachusetts, were the strongholds of the Revolution. It was in the patchwork societies of Pennsylvania and New York that the Tories were strongest.

Among almost all cultural minorities, the proportion of Tories seems to have been clearly higher than among the population at large. The Dutch and Germans seem to have inclined towards supporting the Revolution where they were already anglicized, but not where they had kept their language and separate outlook.[5] In New York, for example, the English-speaking Dutch Reformed congregation was Whiggish, but the Dutch-speaking congregation was Tory, and on such cordial terms with the Anglicans that they were allowed to use St. George's chapel during the British occupation.[6] The Tories praised the loyalty of the French Calvinists at New Rochelle, the only place in the colonies where they had preserved their language, while elsewhere the descendants of the Huguenots were conspicuously active revolutionists.[7]

There seems to have been reason for John Witherspoon's lament that his fellow Scots made bad revolutionists, whether Highlanders in the back country of New York and North Carolina, or Lowlanders along the Virginia and Carolina coast. Even the Ulstermen were tainted with Toryism in the Regulator districts of North Carolina and in the frontier districts of South Carolina.[8] The Loyalism of the Indians is well

[5] See 4 *Am. Arch.* iii. 180; T. G. Tappert, 'Henry Melchior Muhlenberg and the American Revolution', *Church History*, ix. 284–301; K. G. Hamilton, *John Ettwein and the Moravian Church During the Revolutionary Period* (Bethlehem, 1940).

[6] Lydekker, *Life of Inglis*, pp. 195–6.

[7] Jones, *History of New York*, ii. 69.

[8] See J. S. Bassett, 'The Regulators of North Carolina', American Historical Association, *Annual Report*, 1894; and R. Barry, *Mr. Rutledge of South Carolina* (New York, 1942).

known, and contemporary opinion held that the Negroes were
dangerously Toryfied. Of course people like the Brooklyn
Dutch or the South Carolina Germans and Scots may have
remained loyal to Britain partly out of political quietism. It is
difficult not to believe, however, that they were Loyalists also
because they thought Britain would protect them from the
cultural aggression of an Anglo-American majority.

In religion, the lines that divided Tories from Whigs were
quite clearly drawn. Adherents of religious groups that were
in a local minority were everywhere inclined towards Loyalism,
while adherents of the dominant local denomination were
most often Patriots. In New England not many Congregationalists, in the Middle Colonies not many Presbyterians, in
the South not many Episcopalians, were Tories. Conversely,
most of the Anglicans in the North were Tories; so were many
Presbyterians in the Episcopalian South. Of the smaller religious groups, most of the Quakers and German Pietists were
passive Loyalists, and in New England even the Baptists were
accused of 'not being hearty' in the American cause. The
reputation the Methodists had for being poor rebels was perhaps not entirely due to the influence of Wesley and other
English ministers.

The Catholics and Jews apparently form an exception to the
rule that religious minorities leaned towards Toryism. Both
seem generally to have supported the Revolution, although
among the Jews there were notable exceptions like the Hart
family in Newport and the Franks family in Philadelphia.
Jonathan Boucher observed that although the Maryland
Catholics supported the Revolution in its later stages, they had
taken little part at first.[9] It is possible that the Jews and
Catholics were in such suspect and habitual minority, that
they felt obliged to follow what seemed majority opinion for
their own safety.[10]

[9] Boucher, *Causes of the American Revolution*, pp. 241–4.

[10] See J. R. Marcus, *American Jewry: Documents, Eighteenth Century*
(Cincinnati, 1959), pp. 40–46, 232–84; M. A. Ray, *American Opinion of
Roman Catholicism in the Eighteenth Century* (New York, 1936).

Taking all the groups and factions, sects, classes, and inhabitants of regions that seem to have been Tory, they have but on thing in common: they represented conscious minorities, people who felt weak and threatened. The sense of weakness, which is so marked a characteristic of the Tory leaders, is equally evident among the rank and file. Almost all the Loyalists were, in one way or another, more afraid of America than they were of Britain. Almost all of them had interests that they felt needed protection from an American majority. Being fairly certain that they would be in a permanent minority (as Quakers or oligarchs or frontiersmen or Dutchmen) they could not find much comfort in a theory of government that assured them of sovereign equality with other Americans *as individuals*. Not many Loyalists were as explicit in their distrust of individualism as, say, Jonathan Boucher, but most of them shared his suspicion of a political order based on the 'common good' if the common good was to be defined by a numerical majority.

A theory that the Loyalists were compounded of an assortment of minority groups does not, of course, preclude their having in total constituted a majority of Americans. Without the social and religious homogeneity, without the common purpose, and without the organic and efficient leadership of the revolutionists, the Loyalists might still have outnumbered them. In this case the Revolution would have been, as it has sometimes been claimed to have been, the achievement of an organized and wilful minority. The problem of discovering how many Tories there were is complicated, moreover, by there having been, between avowed supporters and avowed opponents of the Revolution, a great middle group of passive citizens who had no clear point of view, who hoped perhaps that one side or the other would win, but who wanted above all not to be disturbed. There must have been many like the New Jersey shopkeeper who stood in his door and prayed that whatever happened, he might have peace in his time. There were probably also a good number of sceptics who thought as

John Ross of Philadelphia did: 'Let who would be king, he well knew that he should be subject.'[11]

An old and symmetrical guess that a third of Americans were revolutionists, another third Loyalists, and a third neutral, has long been accepted by historians as reasonable. It goes back, presumably, to John Adams's assignment of these relative proportions. But Adams may have been trying, unconsciously, to gain distinction for the revolutionists by maintaining they were a wise minority.[12] In Connecticut, the only colony for which anything like an exact estimate of Tory strength has been made, the hard core of Tories seems to have numbered only about six per cent. of the population.[13] But then, Connecticut was one of two or three colonies where the Tories were weakest. During the Revolutionary War perhaps half as many Americans were in arms for the King, at one time or another, as fought on the side of the Congress.[14] Only in New York is it reasonably certain that the Loyalists numbered half the population. Throughout the Middle Colonies, including New York, the Loyalists may have been almost as numerous as their opponents. In the South, however, they could hardly have amounted to more than a fourth or a third of the population, and in New England to scarcely a tenth. A more reasonable guess than Adams's would be that the Loyalists were a third, and the revolutionists two-thirds of the politically active population of the colonies. No reliable estimate is possible until more precise studies of individual colonies have been made.

The outbreak of open war between the British and the Massachusetts militia threw the Tories, temporarily at least, entirely on the defensive. The shock of the news of Lexington and Concord was shortly transformed into anger at those who

[11] Alexander Graydon, *Memoirs of a Life Chiefly Passed in Pennsylvania* (Edinburgh, 1822), p. 115.

[12] Adams, *Works*, x. 87.

[13] See O. Zeichner, *Connecticut's Years of Controversy, 1750–1776* (Chapel Hill, 1949).

[14] H. E. Egerton, *The Causes and Character of the American Revolution* (Oxford, 1923), p. 178.

did not immediately drop all argument and join the fight against the British. Except along the western frontier, and in parts of the Middle Colonies, there was no doubt that Britain and America, not merely Britain and Massachusetts, were at war, and the Tories, who were now calling themselves Loyalists, were beginning to be regarded as traitors. When the news of the Battle of Lexington reached New York, the mob, after almost ten years' confinement, slipped its chains, looted the arsenal, and raged through the streets. While a few weeks earlier it had been said of the New York Whigs that 'no one dares among gentlemen, to support them', it was now possible for John Adams to write, 'The tories put to flight here . . . such a spirit was never seen in New York.'[15]

As the Whigs luxuriated in their sudden release from the bonds of sober argument, they began to look on the Tories with real impatience. To people with a new faith, especially one being forged in the heat of war, the adherents of the old beliefs are either wicked and will not see, or are superstitious and cannot see. George Washington thought the Loyalists were wicked, and denounced them as 'parricides'. Other revolutionists were more charitable, like one who wrote, 'We may say of Toryism as of Popery, that it is always the same. There are worthy individuals among the professors of both; and a few rare instances of real converts from each, through an increase of knowledge, but the prevailing spirit of the parties is uniform and abiding.'[16]

Just after the adjournment of the First Continental Congress, the local committees of inspection had begun to enforce compliance with the Association. In some localities the whole adult population signed the oath. Everywhere it was used to force Tories either to acquiesce in the measures of the Congress, or to declare themselves open 'enemies of American liberty'

[15] John and Abigail Adams, *Familiar Letters*, ed. C. F. Adams (Boston, 1875), p. 54; Becker, *Political Parties*, pp. 193–206; 4 *Am. Arch.* i. 1203; *N.Y. Col. Doc.* viii. 571.
[16] 5 *Am. Arch.* i. 98, 210.

and face ostracism. As a Maryland revolutionist put it, the Association acted 'as a powerful emetick to our Tories'.[17] The efficiency of the committees' work rested on years of experience in informal government, going back in many cases to the committees that had enforced the Non-Importation Agreement in 1768.

The Tories naturally resented what they regarded as the high-handed proceedings of the committees, which they usually compared with the methods of the Inquisition. 'In contending for liberty', one man wrote, 'they seem inclinable to engross it all themselves . . . they are arbitrary and even tyrannical in the whole tenour of their conduct; they allow not to others who differ from them the same liberty of thinking and acting that they claim themselves.'[18] In Massachusetts General Timothy Ruggles and a number of other Loyalists sought to promote a Loyalist Association in opposition to the Congress's oath. The Loyalist oath pledged its signers to defend their 'life, liberty and property', and their 'undoubted right to liberty in eating, drinking, buying, selling; communing, and acting . . . consistent with the laws of God and the King'. Signers promised when one of their number was threatened by 'Committees, mobs, or unlawful assemblies', to arm themselves and go to his aid. Lacking the organization of their opponents, however, the promoters of the Loyalist Association seem not to have had much success.[19]

In New England the social pressure to conform was strong, and opposition to the Revolution was usually individual and verbal. Tories often made abject recantations when they were examined by a committee, like that of William Boltwood:

It evidently appears I have heretofore been unfriendly to my Country; I do hereby publickly acknowledge the offence aforesaid, and ask the forgiveness of all my friends and fellow-countrymen, and promise for the future to act in conjunction with my countrymen, in all ways and methods which shall be judged proper for

17　4 *Am. Arch.* iii. 819.　　　　　　　　　　18　Ibid. ii. 106.
19　Ibid. i. 1057–8; Schlesinger, *Colonial Merchants*, pp. 477–8.

the recovery of the just rights and privileges of the injured Americans, hoping thereby to gain the friendship of my fellow-subjects, which I have most justly forfeited.[20]

Thomas Cowden confessed to 'speaking diminutively of the County Congress at Worcester', and other offences; he was truly sorry and 'ready to convince the world' of the sincerity of his conversion by giving his life, if necessary.[21] William Wheton of Stamford, Connecticut, admitted 'damning the honourable Continental Congress', and 'humbly and heartily' begged the forgiveness of God and of the friends to American liberty.[22]

The Committee of Sheffield, Massachusetts, had John and Job Westover brought before it. John had said the Congress was guilty of rebellion against the King, and Job had said Parliament had a right to tax the colonies. When asked which side they would support in a war between Britain and America, John said it was too difficult a question to answer directly, and Job said he supposed an American victory would be worse for America than a British victory. After a long examination, John 'voluntarily and solemnly' engaged to obey the Continental and Provincial Congresses, and the Committee accepted his declaration as satisfactory. Job, however, was declared an enemy of American liberty and the population was advised to have no dealings with him.[23]

Some recantations were obviously forced, like that of Nahum Willard of Worcester, Massachusetts, who was made to say that he had 'from the perverseness of a wicked heart, maliciously and scandalously abused' the Congress, the Selectmen of the town of Worcester, and committees in general. He admitted to being a wicked liar and an enemy to American liberty.[24]

People with influence could appeal against a local committee's decision. The Selectmen of Waltham, Massachusetts, found

[20] 4 Am. Arch. iii. 145.   [21] Ibid. 322.
[22] Ibid. 692.   [23] Ibid. ii. 545.
[24] Ibid. iii. 463.

Abijah Brown guilty of having belittled the general of the Massachusetts army and the committeemen as 'a set of idiots and lunaticks'. But the Provincial Committee of Safety restored him to favour on the grounds that he had temporarily fallen under the influence of 'disaffected antagonists'.[25] Occasionally the revolutionists would run into unexpected opposition, as when the Committee of New Ipswich, New Hampshire, instructed David Hills, a shopkeeper, to reduce his prices. Hills refused, charged the Committee with being arbitrary, and, worst of all, claimed that two leading members of the Committee itself had privately declared against the present proceedings of the colonies, and had said it would have been better to comply with Parliament's requisitions.[26]

Sometimes the local committees themselves lacked the proper spirit. The Portsmouth, New Hampshire, Committee was severely criticized by warm patriots for having arranged to supply a British sloop lying below the town with fresh beef in return for being allowed to bring fresh fish into Portsmouth.[27]

The tug of economic self-interest could be exquisitely sharp. When Stephen Parker of Machias, on the Maine coast, was accused of trading with Nova Scotia in violation of the Association, he apologized to the Council and House of Representatives of Massachusetts Bay in the following words: 'May it please your Honours: Ignorance, inadvertence, and absolute necessity, were the sole cause of my setting foot in the Government of Nova-Scotia.'[28]

One of the most troublesome cases of disaffection in New England was that of Governor Joseph Wanton of Rhode Island. His Toryism was embarrassing since he was not a 'fawning Courtier' like the royal governors, but the duly elected head of a 'perfect Democracy'. Nevertheless, in May 1775 he raised the ghost of Newport's detestable cosmopolitanism by urging the General Assembly of Rhode Island to avoid the 'horrours and calamities of a civil war'. He expressed an ardent

25 4 *Am. Arch.* ii. 720–1.   26 Ibid. 1711–13.
27 Ibid. iii. 59.   28 Ibid. vi. 443.

desire to see a union between Great Britain and her colonies upon an 'equitable, permanent basis', and advised the Assembly to negotiate separately with Parliament. He said that Rhode Island's happiness and prosperity were founded on its connexion with Britain; 'if once we are separated,' he asked, 'where shall we find another Britain to supply our loss?' The Assembly promptly forbade the oath of office to be administered to Governor Wanton, and provided for the commissioning of militia officers without his signature.[29]

Little escaped the notice of the committees and congresses: the self-constituted General Court of Massachusetts, in the midst of its efforts to raise an army, found time to recommend to the Corporation and Overseers of Harvard College that they 'inquire into the principles' of members of their faculty and dismiss any instructors who appeared to be unfriendly to American liberty. They were also urged not to appoint any teachers, 'but such whose political principles they can confide in'.[30]

The only opposition to the Revolution in New England which threatened to be dangerous was in western Connecticut.[31] The New Haven Town Meeting passed a resolution opposing the taking up of arms. The Ridgefield and Danbury Meetings passed resolutions condemning the measures of the Congress. In a number of towns, among them Reading and New Milford, Loyalist oaths were sworn to by a majority of the inhabitants. The Connecticut Assembly was informed in May 1775 that the 'major part' of a militia company in Waterbury, 'both Officers and Soldiers', was 'totally disaffected to the general cause of American liberty, and that they altogether refuse to adopt the

[29] Ibid. ii. 472, 662–3.
[30] Ibid. iii. 1451.
[31] The Tories of Worcester County, Massachusetts, were 'having frequent meetings in large bodies' in July 1776, but there was no actual insurrection. Collective opposition to the Congress in Massachusetts usually took the form of passive non-co-operation, as when the Barnstable Town Meeting voted (Jan. 1775) against purchasing arms, encouraging the Minutemen, or sending delegates to the Provincial Congress; it endorsed the Association, however. 4 *Am. Arch.* i. 1093, 1250–1.

measures advised by the Continental Congress'. This threat
was overcome by a promptly and secretly organized expedition
of several hundred Whig militiamen from the eastern part of
the province who disarmed all the Loyalists in the area around
Fairfield and took a dozen Tory leaders prisoner. One Whig
wrote with modest satisfaction, 'Our people made them rise
about three o'clock in the morning, when there was the greatest
confusion imaginable.' The Connecticut Loyalists were caught
unprepared and made no resistance, though some escaped
across the Sound to Long Island.[32]

In New York the Assembly had been prorogued after it sent
its petition to Britain. Before it could meet again, a 'Provincial
Congress' had been elected by mass acclamation from a list of
nominees put up by the New York Committee. The Provincial
Congress brought New York back into the Revolution by
appointing delegates to the Continental Congress and taking
over the powers of government in New York. Compared with
similar irregular congresses in the other provinces, the New
York Congress followed a moderate course. It simply resumed
the customary practice of the New York conservatives of trying
to control the Revolutionary movement by discreet participa-
tion in it.

The day after the news of the Battle of Lexington arrived,
Lord North's 'Conciliatory Propositions' in answer to the
earlier petition of the Assembly, reached New York. To the
disappointment of the conservatives, it rejected the Assembly's
Memorial. North's Propositions did suggest, instead of outright parliamentary taxation of the colonies, a return to a
modified system of requisition, by which Parliament, rather
than the Crown, would lay its demands before the colonial
assemblies.[33] Ten years before, this might have been acceptable,
but in the circumstances no attention was paid to it, and the
conservatives were no longer able to hold out high hopes of

---

[32] 4 *Am. Arch.* i. 1202, 1216, 1259–60, 1270; ii. 575; iii. 852; Gipson, *Jared
Ingersoll*, p. 337; Zeichner, *Connecticut*, pp. 182–6, 198–217, 226–35.
[33] Becker, *Political Parties*, pp. 197–203.

British conciliation. It was not the first time that Parliament had helped the revolutionists convince America that nothing could be expected from Britain.

The New York Committee and the Provincial Congress both did their best to keep the Revolution from getting out of hand. After the Battle of Lexington the New York Committee advised the people to keep cool, and not deal so harshly with the Tories as to make outright enemies of them. 'In short, gentlemen,' the Committee's address said, 'consider that our contest is for liberty; and therefore we should be extremely cautious how we permit our struggles to hurry us into acts of violence and extravagance inconsistent with freedom'.[34] The Provincial Congress wrote the New York delegates to the Continental Congress urging them to try for a reconciliation, and observed that 'such controversies as we are now engaged in frequently end in the demolition of those rights and privileges which they were instituted to defend'.[35]

The middle road which the New Yorkers were still trying to follow demanded sometimes the drawing of fine distinctions. When in June 1775 the royal governor of New York and General Washington entered New York on the same day on different errands, both received escorts from the Provincial Congress, which instructed a militia colonel to 'have the residue of his Battalion ready to receive either the General or Governor Tryon, whichever shall first arrive, and to wait on both as well as circumstances will allow'. Both Tryon and Washington were cheered in the streets, perhaps by the same crowds.[36]

New York was regarded with suspicion in the other colonies, particularly in New England. A Connecticut man wrote to a friend in New York that it had been said 'your Province would desert us'. He advised the New Yorkers to take care. 'It is no time now to dally, or be merely neutral; he that is not

---

[34] 4 *Am. Arch.* ii. 427.
[35] Ibid. 1329.
[36] Becker, *Political Parties*, p. 218; A. Nevins, *The American States During and After the Revolution, 1775–1789* (New York, 1924), p. 87.

for us is against us. . . . If you desert, our men will as cheerfully attack New-York as Boston, for we can but perish.'[37]

General David Wooster, then commanding a small number of Continental troops around New York, wrote to the governor of his own province of Connecticut recalling the 'suspicious light in which the New-York Congress are viewed by the rest of the Continent', and begging that he would not have to serve under them. Wooster had so little confidence in the New Yorkers that he took to sending the 'most Obnoxious' Tories to Connecticut for safe keeping.[38] More direct Connecticut aggression against New York occurred in November 1775 when Isaac Sears rode in with a troop of Connecticut irregulars and destroyed Rivington's press, thus silencing the last press in the colonies open to the Tories. Sears and his men also took a number of New York Tories back to Connecticut as prisoners, including Samuel Seabury. They deposited Seabury and Rivington's type in New Haven and concluded the day 'in festivity and innocent mirth'.[39] In New York even good Whigs like Philip Schuyler and John Jay were annoyed, and the New York Committee petitioned the Provincial Congress protesting the interference of one colony in another's affairs.[40]

The New Englanders were right, however, in thinking the Revolution in New York needed outside help. Only in a few parts of the province, principally Suffolk County (the eastern half of Long Island, settled mainly by New Englanders), part of Ulster County, and the city of New York, could the committees take the kind of coercive action against individual

[37] 4 *Am. Arch.* ii. 363.

[38] Ibid. iii. 89, 134–5, 263. One of these was the Reverend James Lyon, a Church of England rector at Southold, Long Island. Wooster wrote that Lyon was 'a man of infamous character, but a pretty sensible fellow, . . . the main spring of all the tories on that part of Long-Island . . . able to do great mischief'. Lyon was entrusted to the care of the Committee of Hartford, Connecticut.

[39] Frank Moore, *Diary of the American Revolution from Newspapers and Original Documents* (Hartford, 1876), pp. 173–5; Seabury, *Letters of a Westchester Farmer*, p. 148.

[40] 4 *Am. Arch.* iii. 1675–6; iv. 185–6.

Tories that was commonplace in New England. Even then there were few recantations, and the committees' action was usually mild.[41] Much of the opposition to the Revolution in New York was collective, sometimes involving whole counties.[42] A number of town meetings passed Loyalist resolutions, and many localities refused to send delegates to the Provincial Congress. When, for example, several hundred Westchester County Whigs met at White Plains to choose delegates to the Congress, a much larger number of Tories appeared, denounced the meeting, and marched off singing 'the grand and animating song of "God save great George our King" '.[43]

Peter De Witt wrote that in Dutchess County, 'all are tories, only a few excepted'. The Loyalists went about armed, interfered with the selection of militia officers, 'damned the Congress', and enlisted young men in the British service. The most energetic Tories were the local rivermen, who once threatened to come with an armed vessel and carry off the leading Whigs to the British, and who, until their boats were burnt, were active in taking men down-river to serve with the British.[44] In October 1775 the New York Congress was informed of a conspiracy 'of a great number of people' in the lower Hudson Valley to join the King's troops, and some Loyalists around Peekskill attempted to arm against the Congress, but were disarmed by the local militia.[45]

[41] The Committee of Pownalborough charged Abiel Wood, a selectman of the town, with having said that the members of the Continental Congress 'drank thirty bumpers of wine a piece before they passed their Resolves', and that the Resolves would ruin the country. He had also called the officers of the Continental Army rebels and traitors. He had distributed and praised Chandler's pamphlets, and had said that most of the members of the Provincial Congress were 'damned villains'. He was declared an enemy to his country. 4 Am. Arch. iii. 151–3.

In New York City, Thomas Pratt was accused of having threatened to set fire to the town if the Connecticut troops should come in. He was reprimanded. Ibid. 1263–4.

John Cock of Yonkers, a militia captain, 'damned the Provincial Congress', and his commission was taken away from him. Ibid. 902–3.

[42] See Flick, *Loyalism in New York*, pp. 58–94.

[43] 4 Am. Arch. ii. 321–2.   [44] Ibid. iii. 458–9, 466.   [45] Ibid. 1305, 1763.

The adjoining part of New Jersey suspended dealings with Staten Island because the inhabitants 'have manifested an unfriendly disposition towards the liberties of America'. Staten Island sent no delegates to the Provincial Congress, and its people were accused of continuing to trade with the British in defiance of the Association. The Staten Island Committee of Safety itself was accused of favouring men brought before it as Tories. One Whig complained that the Committee allowed the men he had accused to call him 'an informer, cut-throat, dirty rascal, dirty dog, liar, &c.' in their presence, and then dismissed them.[46]

The most serious opposition to the Revolution in New York was on the Atlantic and Appalachian frontiers, respectively: in Queen's County on Long Island, and in Tryon County.[47] Disaffection in Tryon County was the more menacing. The fur trading empire of Sir William Johnson had passed on to his son, Colonel Guy Johnson, who from his capital at Albany could raise the Indians as far as the Great Lakes for a war on the settlers. In addition to his Indians, Colonel Johnson had staunch allies in Sir John Johnson and the Highland Scots settled in Tryon County. In May 1775 Colonel Johnson warned the New York Congress that if the rumoured plan to imprison him was carried out, the Indians would take it as a hostile act and attack the frontier settlements. He offered to observe neutrality if left alone. Receiving no reply, he denounced the Congress and disappeared into the Indian country.

The Highlanders were well armed, and there were rumours that they planned to join the Indians and march down the Hudson Valley, raising the local Tories as they went. In January 1776, however, General Philip Schuyler took several thousand militiamen into Tryon County in a surprise march and disarmed the 'malignant' Scots, taking everything from their dirks and claymores to several four- and six-pound

---

[46] 4 *Am. Arch.* i. 1234–5; iii. 624–5; v. 136–7.
[47] Tryon County at this time included much of upstate New York, while Queen's County included most of the western half of Long Island.

cannon. Six hostages for the Scots' future good behaviour were sent prisoners to Pennsylvania. The Indians were still hoping to remain neutral and did nothing, so the immediate threat of a Loyalist rising on the frontier was dispelled.[48]

Queen's County was not only maritime, but also it was on the cultural frontier between New England and the Middle Colonies. The anti-New-England feelings of its people were genuine and obdurate. The Queen's County towns had refused to send delegates to the Provincial Congress and had passed Loyalist resolutions instead. The man who had been chosen to represent the county in the Provincial Congress did not attend, and explained that since 'the people seemed to be much inclined to remain peaceable and quiet', he thought it would be presumptuous of him to claim to represent them. In the November 1775 elections for the Provincial Congress, the freeholders of Queen's County voted 788 to 221 not to send any deputies at all. In December a great number of the county's inhabitants signed a declaration of neutrality, in which they said they had 'carefully avoided every ostentatious display' of their sentiments, but had reluctantly been compelled to arm themselves against threats of violence. They said they wanted only to remain in peace.

The Continental Congress could not afford to allow the development of a neutrality movement, and therefore decided to make an example of Queen's County. It issued a declaration virtually outlawing the county and denouncing its people for being 'incapable of resolving to live and die freemen'. The Congress resolved that the Loyalists should be disarmed and the 'dangerous' ones confined, and that the names of all dissidents in the county should be published throughout America. All the inhabitants of Queen's County were instructed not to leave the county without a passport issued by the New York

[48] 4 *Am. Arch.* ii. 661–2, 1669; iii. 660–1; iv. 668, 818–29. The Six Nations tried to stay neutral: 'we bear an equal proportion of love to you, and the others over the great waters', they wrote to the Congress. The Mohawks warned the Whigs, however, that they and Sir John Johnson were 'of one blood'. Ibid. iii. 86, 478–9; iv. 683.

Committee of Safety. At the same time as this declaration was issued, a large force of Continental troops was sent in. Lacking any encouragement from the British, the Tories finally allowed themselves to be disarmed without a fight.[49]

Thus by prompt action New York's revolutionists, aided by New Englanders, had secured the two hostile frontiers, mountain and maritime, which in New York were so dangerously close together. The Tories continued to form 'barbarous and infernal plots' and drink 'Damnation to the Congress', but for the time being they were disorganized and helpless.[50] Disaffection in New York did not disappear, but it took more and more the form of passive non-co-operation. This is evident from the difficulty which the new Provincial Congress found in getting a quorum in November 1775. Although the Congress was to have convened on 14 November, by 22 November only four of the twelve counties in the province had sent delegates. The Congress finally met on 6 December, with delegates present from only five counties. New York was waiting to see how the war went.[51]

New Jersey had not played an active part in the revolutionary movement, and was inclined to take its lead from New York or, preferably, from Pennsylvania. The New Jersey Tories, although they preferred neutrality to insurrection, made up perhaps a greater part of the population than in any of the thirteen colonies except New York and Georgia. There were, however, a number of localities which had been settled by New Englanders and were vigorously Whig. The New Jersey revolutionists made up in energy what they lacked in numbers, and maintained a strict discipline over dissidents in areas they controlled. For example, a Quibbletown cooper

---

[49] 4 *Am. Arch.* ii. 251, 273–4, 1114–15; iii. 795, 1389–92; iv. 203–4, 858–61, 1630–1. On 2 Jan. 1776 the Continental Congress resolved to disarm all Tories, 'such unworthy Americans as, regardless of their duty to their Creator, their country and their posterity, have taken part with our oppressors'. Committees were to imprison the 'more dangerous'. Ibid. 1629.

[50] Ibid. v. 450; vi. 1054.

[51] Ibid. iii. 1751 ff.; Becker, *Political Parties*, pp. 234–6.

who had reviled the local committee and the Continental Congress, was stripped naked, 'well coated with tar and feathers' and taken round the village in a cart. A local patriot wrote that this ceremony was conducted 'with that regularity and decorum that ought to be observed in all public punishments'.[52]

The British government had an unusually tenacious champion in New Jersey in the person of the royal governor, William Franklin. Whether or not he was, as his father, Benjamin, maintained, a 'thorough Courtier', Franklin proved himself an unbending Tory. With little encouragement from England, he had done his best to keep New Jersey out of the Revolution. Although he was unable in May 1775 to persuade the Assembly to negotiate separately with Britain, he continued to nurture Tory sentiment in the province. His was the guiding hand behind the petitions which the New Jersey Assembly received in the autumn of 1775, praying that it 'discourage an Independency on Great Britain'. The Assembly replied that reports of independence were groundless, but it nevertheless instructed the New Jersey delegates to the Continental Congress 'utterly to reject any propositions, if such should be made, that may separate this Colony from the Mother Country'. Prodded by Franklin, the Assembly finally overcame its scruples at acting separately from the other colonies, and drafted a petition to the King, 'humbly beseeching him to . . . prevent the effusion of blood; and to express the great desire this House hath to a restoration of peace and harmony'.[53]

Before this petition could be adopted, however, a committee led by John Jay and John Dickinson 'came in great haste' from the Continental Congress and harangued the Assembly on the danger to the American cause of one colony acting separately from the others. Moved by Dickinson's skilful pleading, the Assembly was finally persuaded to drop its petition. Franklin wrote to Lord Dartmouth in despair that, although he was still

[52] 4 *Am. Arch.* iv. 203.
[53] Ibid. ii. 595, 599–601; iii. 1854–7.

convinced the majority of people in New Jersey were 'greatly averse to an Independency', he feared independence would be achieved by degrees, and in such a way that the people would not realize what was happening until it was too late to act.[54] Franklin stubbornly held his ground against rising opposition until June 1776 when the New Jersey Provincial Congress had him arrested. He stiffly reaffirmed his loyalty to the King, which, he said, it 'has been the Pride of my Life to demonstrate upon all Occasions'. He was judged a virulent and dangerous enemy to America and was sent to Connecticut, where he was held in close confinement.[55]

In Pennsylvania Galloway's desertion of the Continental Congress had been generally disapproved, and there was little overt Tory activity in 1775. Although, like so many New Yorkers, some of the men of property in Pennsylvania supported the Congress for fear of mob violence, many still supported resistance to Britain out of a genuine attachment to ideas of liberty. Pennsylvania's characteristic attitude seems to have lain somewhere between the calculating cosmopolitanism of New York and the libertarian pride of Virginia. Only a 'perverse, drivelling knot of Quakers' held out with quiet obstinacy against the Congress. The Quakers had deliberately embarrassed the Massachusetts delegates at the First Continental Congress by asking them pointedly about liberty of conscience in New England. When John Adams had tried to justify Massachusetts's laws against the Quakers, Israel Pemberton had said, 'Oh, sir, don't urge liberty of conscience in favour of such laws!'

In 1775 the Philadelphia Friends Meeting sent letters to Quakers all through the Middle Colonies recommending nonparticipation in all measures of rebellion, and urging them 'constantly to remember, that to fear God, honour the King, and do good to all men, is our indispensable duty'. The Quakers prayed that nothing should break the 'happy con-

---

[54] 4 *Am. Arch.* iii. 1871–5.
[55] Ibid. vi. 1629; *N.J. Archives*, 1st series, x. 698–701.

nexion' the colonies had with England, 'or tend to introduce persecution and suffering among us'. 'It is not our business', the Philadelphia Meeting decided, to set up governments, 'much less to plot and contrive the ruin or overturn of any of them.' In these ambitious times, for the Quakers alone, the words of Jesus, 'My kingdom is not of this world', had pre-scriptive meaning.[56]

John Adams thought Maryland was an 'eccentrick Colony'. The Marylanders at the First Congress had usually voted with the Virginians, but had changed sides to support Galloway's Plan. The internal politics of Maryland seem to have been less turbulent in the years before the Revolution, and relations with the British government less strained, than in perhaps any other colony. In addition, some of Maryland's eccentricity may be explained by the partition of the colony by Chesa-peake Bay. The Eastern Shore was maritime, in hostile com-petition with New England, and Tory. The tobacco-growing regions on the western side of the bay were Whig, although, to be sure, living there was one of the most vexatious Tories in the thirteen colonies, that combative advocate of the Church of England, the Reverend Jonathan Boucher.

Boucher had, by his own account, acted as a political manager for Governor Eden and had attempted to handle the Mary-land Assembly for him. He had also, as mentioned above, tried to bring the Maryland and Virginia clergy into a common political programme with the Northern clergy, and had in his sermons and writings generally 'endeavoured . . . to check the immense mischief that was impending'. Though bumptious and self-important, Boucher was a man of energy and ability, and had become as obnoxious to Maryland Whigs as Governor Franklin was to those in New Jersey. Finally, after preaching for six months with two loaded pistols lying ready on his pulpit cushion, Boucher was persuaded to leave the colony in order to avoid mob violence. He wrote sadly that his friends

---

[56] 4 *Am. Arch.* i. 1093–4; iii. 1777–9; iv. 785–7; Adams, *Works*, ii. 397–400.

were 'as strongly for my flying as I alone was for my not flying'.[57]

More serious politically, though perhaps less serious philosophically than Boucher's disaffection, was that of the Tories of the Eastern Shore. With the possible exception of western Long Island, the Chesapeake peninsula had the highest proportion of Loyalists in the colonies. They seem to have been fairly evenly distributed through the nine Eastern Shore counties of Maryland, the two southern Delaware counties, and the two Virginia counties at the tip of the peninsula. There were reports of imminent Tory insurrections in each of these counties at one time or another during 1775 and the early part of 1776.

In Worcester County, Maryland, a local committee reported in the autumn of 1775 that the friends of liberty there were in a 'very melancholy situation'. They said they had no ammunition, and 'the Tories exceed our number'. The Loyalists were getting arms from a British ship, which they had heard intended to give direct assistance if a sufficient number of signatures to a Loyalist Association was obtained. A Whig officer who was invited to help drill a newly formed militia company found they had their own articles of association. They asked him how he liked them. He replied cautiously that they were something like the articles of his own company, 'they were for their King and Country'. 'Yes,' said one of the militiamen, 'but we are against Boston.' And they 'all huzzaed for the King, and pulled off their hats'.[58]

One day in September 1775, when a Somerset County, Maryland, militia company met for drill, part of the company drew up as usual, but 'one-half or more' drew apart under a certain Isaac Atkinson, and put on red cockades instead of the usual black. Atkinson had ordered his men to bring sharp flints in their guns, and when asked if he meant to oppose the Congress, said he did, 'and offered to lay Mr. Whitear a doubloon he

---

[57] Boucher, *Reminiscences*, pp. 104–5, 113, 128–30.
[58] 4 *Am. Arch.* iii. 1574–6.

would by that day week have three hundred men to join him in the opposition'. One of his men said, 'Yes, five hundred; for he is the only man that had opened their eyes, and [he] ought to be upheld.' Atkinson said 'that it was rebellion the way the people of Boston were going on, and that he believed the people of Boston wanted a King of their own in America'. He said the present dispute was about religion, 'and was a Presbyterian scheme', and 'a day must be appointed, and they must fight it out'. No day was appointed, however.[59]

There were reports in the spring of 1776 of a thousand Loyalists under arms in Sussex County, Delaware, and some local Whigs wrote that unless troops were sent in to protect them, 'we must be candid enough to inform you, that self-preservation will oblige us either to leave . . . or fall in and run with the current, either of which will be hateful to us'. In Caroline and Dorchester Counties, Maryland, several companies of militia had laid down their arms. In Newcastle County, Delaware, the people were in contact with British ships in the Delaware and were furnishing them with provisions. Some Maryland Whig militiamen who had been sent 'to the assistance of the people' in Accomack and Northampton Counties, Virginia, at the southern tip of the Chesapeake peninsula, reported that they would have little assistance *from* the people, should they need it.[60]

The situation in the Chesapeake country, as well as across Delaware Bay in southern New Jersey, where the people 'would much rather have the Regulars than the Yankees',[61] was clearly alarming. Yet, as on Long Island, the Loyalists finally lost heart and allowed themselves to be disarmed. They were not confident of getting assistance from the British and, although

[59] Ibid. 1571-4, 1576, 1582, 1585.
[60] Ibid. iv. 753, 1522; vi. 804-5, 808, 833; 5th series, i. 10.
[61] Loyalist insurrections were reported imminent in Monmouth, Hunterdon, and Bergen Counties, New Jersey in June 1776, and Whig militiamen could not be persuaded to go near the Deal Shore in southern New Jersey for fear the people would turn them over to the British. Ibid. 4th series, vi. 1630; 5th series, i. 602-3.

they were not afraid of the local Whigs, they were impressed by the reputed strength of the revolutionists inland.[62]

In Virginia, except for the two isolated counties on the Chesapeake peninsula, the Tories were most numerous along the coast near Norfolk, and in the sparsely settled counties beyond the Blue Ridge in the West. Many of the coastal Tories were Scots merchants and small planters. The Scots formed an energetic, if often unpopular, part of the population of Virginia, and though not as numerous as the Chesapeake and New Jersey Loyalists, caused much more trouble. Perhaps because many of them were native Britons, they were willing at an early date to take up arms against the Revolution. They obtained supplies from the British naval forces off the coast and fought several small engagements with the Whigs late in 1775. When finally forced to give up Norfolk, they continued to operate from British ships.[63]

The Loyalists on the western frontier of Virginia were mixed Scots, Indians, and Americans, like those in upper New York. Their leader was Major John Connolly, an American who had served with the British in the West Indies during the Seven Years War, and afterwards settled beyond the mountains in West Augusta County in a region still in dispute between Virginia and Pennsylvania. In August 1775 Connolly had made his way across Virginia to Portsmouth where he acquainted the royal governor, Lord Dunmore, with his plans for a general rising of the Indians, French, and Tories of the Appalachian country. Connolly thought that he could stay the winter at Detroit and come up the Ohio in the spring of 1776 with a few regular troops, gather his Loyalists and take Fort Pitt. General Gage authorized him to offer three hundred acres of land to every man who would join him. Connolly hoped that after taking Fort Pitt he could march across Virginia, perhaps enlisting discontented indentured servants, and meet Dunmore

---

[62] 4 *Am. Arch.* 4th series, iii. 1585; iv. 719–21; v. 1515; vi. 833.

[63] Ibid. ii. 1691–2; iii. 92–96, 1072–3; vi. 686; H. J. Eckenrode, *The Revolution in Virginia* (Boston, 1916), pp. 58, 84, 91.

at Alexandria. This ambitious scheme, the first part of which may have been feasible, collapsed when Connolly and two Scots friends were arrested by the militia at Frederick, Maryland, on their way back to the West.[64]

North Carolina was a poor province, thinly populated and less active politically than Virginia or South Carolina. Perhaps the most vigorous elements in the population were the New Englanders in the Piedmont and the Scots and English along the coast. There were a good many Scots Loyalists at Wilmington and around Cape Fear, although they were outnumbered by native planters of South Carolina origin.[65] Janet Schaw, a Scotswoman who was visiting relatives in North Carolina in 1775, wrote a vivid account of the plight of the Scots Tories at Wilmington: 'An officer or committeeman enters a plantation with his posse. The Alternative is proposed, Agree to join us, and your persons and properties are safe; . . . But if you refuse, we are directly to cut up your corn, shoot your pigs, burn your houses, seize your Negroes and perhaps tar and feather yourself.'[66]

White Loyalists were not the only enemies of the Revolution in the South. The Whigs were in constant terror of Negro insurrection. There seem to have been some grounds for what a Whig in one of Crèvecœur's *Sketches* said to a Negro boy: 'They say you are a good fellow, only a little Toryfied like most of your colour.'[67] Wherever British ships appeared off the coast in the South, Negroes would row out with provisions, and often Negro men would stay as volunteers. Many Americans were shocked at the fraternization between the British and the Negroes. An American prisoner aboard a British ship in Delaware Bay observed indignantly that three Negro men

[64] 'Narrative of John Connolly, Loyalist', *Pennsylvania Magazine of History and Biography*, xii. 310–24, 407–20; xiii. 61–70, 153–67, 281–91; 4 *Am. Arch.* iii. 1047–8.

[65] See R. O. DeMond, *The Loyalists in North Carolina During the Revolution* (Durham, 1940).

[66] Janet Schaw, *Journal of a Lady of Quality*, ed. E. W. Andrews (New Haven, 1921), pp. 195 ff.   [67] Crèvecœur, *Sketches*, p. 310.

who had come aboard 'were shaken hands with, and kindly received and entertained' by the English, who promised them their freedom when the rebellion was over. British prisoners in New Jersey were accused of 'continually plotting with the Negroes'.[68]

In the spring of 1776 the North Carolina Congress recommended that all masters and owners of slaves on the south side of the Cape Fear River 'remove such male slaves as are capable of bearing arms, or otherwise assisting the enemy, into the country, remote from the sea'. Janet Schaw wrote that the Negroes were going off to the woods around Wilmington. The whites, she said, were all in arms, 'the patroles going thro' all the town', and searching the Negroes' houses to see that they were all at home by nine at night. She wrote that one Negro was shot and killed by a nervous Whig, but that there was no insurrection, for one reason because the Negroes had no arms.[69]

In some of the western counties of North Carolina many former Regulators were Loyalists. Being old rebels themselves, the Regulators were sceptical of the sudden zeal for liberty of the lowland planters, whom they distrusted more than the British. In an effort to conciliate the Regulators, the North Carolina Provincial Council appointed a committee to 'explain the proceedings of the Congress' to the back country, 'where the People are not well informed', and had been misled by Tory pamphlets distributed by Governor Martin. The explanations were apparently insufficient, because in February 1776 some 1,600 Regulators and Scots Highlanders gathered

---

[68] 4 *Am. Arch.* vi. 811, 1639. Three hundred Negroes took part, with 250 British and 150 Virginia Scots Loyalists, in a landing on Gwin's Island in the Delaware in June 1776. Georgia Negroes were reported running away to join the British. Negroes in southern New Jersey were reported arming themselves. Ibid. 811; 5th series, i. 7, 16.

In March 1776 Lord Dunmore organized an 'Ethiopian Corps', which saw service later in the war. There were many accounts like that of a Marylander who wrote: 'A valuable Negro made his escape from us [to the British] last night, he not being so well guarded as he ought to have been.' Ibid. i. 518; ii. 160.   [69] Ibid. 4th series, v. 1355; Schaw, *Journal*, pp. 200–1.

in arms under the King's standard at Cross Creek. At Moore's Creek Bridge the Loyalists, under the temporary command of Colonel Alexander McLeod, found a smaller force of Whigs in entrenched positions, and the Scots charged them before the Regulators were ready. The Whigs repelled the charge, and the Loyalists fled the field. Most of them were disarmed, and their leaders taken prisoner, soon after.[70]

The back country of South Carolina was even more disaffected than that of North Carolina. In the summer of 1775 the Charleston oligarchs sent William Drayton and the Reverend William Tennent, Charleston's leading dissenting minister, on a mission to District Ninety-Six 'to explain to the People the causes of the present disputes'. At first they made little headway with the Tory leaders. Tennent wrote, 'We soon found the unchangeable malignity of their minds, and the inexpressible pains they are at to blind the people, and fill them with bitterness against the gentlemen, as they are called.' Tennent had, however, true missionary zeal. He and Drayton talked for hours with the principal Tory leader, Thomas Fletchall: 'We humoured him—we laughed with him; then we recurred to argument, remonstrances, and entreaties, to join his Country, and all America.' At first, all Fletchall would say was that 'he would never take up arms against his King or his countrymen, and that the Proceedings of the Congress at Philadelphia were impolitick, disrespectful, and irritating to the King'.

Finally, however, Fletchall agreed to sign a 'Treaty of Neutrality' with Drayton and Tennent. This included a qualified admission of the authority of the Provincial Congress, which the other Tory leaders refused to make. In November 1775, with Fletchall and his men neutral, fighting broke out between the Whig militia and the Tories led by Robert Cunningham. Cunningham's men, though numerically superior

---

[70] 4 *Am. Arch.* ii. 116–17, 271–2; iii. 190, 679, 1093; iv. 306, 981–3, 1488; v. 61–63; DeMond, *Loyalists in North Carolina*, pp. 94–96; M. Jensen, *The Articles of Confederation* (Madison, 1940), pp. 25–26.

to the Whigs, were defeated and disarmed. Drayton ascribed the Tory defeat to lack of leadership, and wrote that if the royal governor, William Campbell, had gone into the back country in the summer of 1775 and led the Tories himself, the 'whole proceedings' of the Provincial Congress might have been overthrown. Campbell, however, had stayed in Charleston, there 'to experience the daily loss of his executive powers; and the little consideration in which he was holden'. The Whigs sealed their victory over the Tories by a generous amnesty in March 1776, by which time many Tories were fighting alongside the Whigs against the Cherokees.[71]

The Indians had been incited to attack the settlements by John Stuart, a South Carolina Tory who was the royal superintendent of Indian affairs in the South. Stuart had a scheme similar to Connolly's for raising the frontiersmen and Indians, and General Gage had apparently hoped to concert both plans with a rising led in upper New York by Guy Johnson. Stuart did persuade the Cherokees to make a general attack in the Carolinas, but the whole plan miscarried when the Indians massacred Tories as well as Whigs. This changed the 'countenance and tone' of some of the Loyalists, a number of whom offered their services to the Charleston government and fought the Indians. The Cherokees were driven back into the mountains, and the active Loyalists were reduced, for the time being, to a few marauding bands.[72]

[71] 4 *Am. Arch.* ii. 1715–16; iii. 180–2, 214–17, 1606; iv. 215–16, 306, 950; v. 592.

[72] 5 *Am. Arch.* i. 481, 610; ii. 209; *N.Y. Col. Doc.* viii. 159; Samuel Curwen, *Journal and Letters* (New York, 1845), pp. 659–60.

In Georgia, as in Nova Scotia, the very small population was too dependent on British subsidies and protection to be able to afford revolution. Georgia Whigs reported to the Continental Congress that there was little enthusiasm for non-intercourse with Britain in Savannah. 'There were some . . . virtuously for the measures; others strenuously against them; but more who called themselves neutrals than either.' In March 1776, when Georgia was about to resume trade with Britain, the South Carolina Congress sent troops to occupy Savannah. 4 *Am. Arch.* ii. 280; v. 585.

For Stuart, see J. R. Alden, *John Stuart and the Southern Colonial Frontier* (Ann Arbor, 1944).

Everywhere then, in 1775, the Tories were intimidated, disarmed, and defeated, even in districts where they had overwhelming local superiority. Lack of organization, of course, contributed to their failure. This is clear, for example, in the absence of any co-ordination of the several abortive western risings. Had a concerted attack by Tories and Indians been made all along the frontier from New York to Georgia, it might have proved embarrassing to the Congress. Here, however, not only their lack of organization, but also the inherent disparateness of the Tories handicapped them. The alliance between the Cherokees and the South Carolina frontiersmen was uneasy if not unsound. In North Carolina the Regulators and Scots Highlanders mistrusted each other, and none of the frontier Tories had much in common with the stolid farmers of Long Island, or the Chesapeake fishermen.

The Tories were willing enough to fight for their principles and prejudices, as they showed later in the war. But separate grievances can make common cause only when they have a common standard to rally around. The failure, in years gone by, of Tory leaders to provide such a standard was decisive now. In 1775 only the British could have given leadership to the various Tory groups, supplied and reinforced them, and led them into common purpose; this the British were as yet unwilling to attempt. Thus the Loyalist ranks succumbed to the same lack of confidence and direction that had for twenty years unnerved the Tory leaders.

CHAPTER VI

The True Whigs

LIKE all true revolutions, the American Revolution had a hard simplicity of purpose, an inner cohesion that gave it irresistible momentum. It was as if the forces of the Revolution formed one body, one soul, as John Adams wrote, '. . . one great, wise, active and noble spirit', while the forces in opposition to it spoke with a thousand tongues and held together scarcely better than sand. The Revolution seemed privileged to meet each of its enemies separately, perhaps simply because they were separate. And, by a secret logic of its history, the Revolution sought out and destroyed its weakest enemies first. Thus the New England Tories, whose establishment was all on the surface, with no roots in the stony soil underneath, were the first to be shattered. Next the numerous, but leaderless and inchoate, groups of Tories throughout the other colonies were subdued and disciplined by congress and committee. And then, before having to face the gathered armies of England, the Revolution turned to deal sharply with those of its own supporters who misunderstood its meaning.

The Second Continental Congress appeared to be, if any different, a more conservative body than the First. A clear majority of its members were opposed to American independence and hopeful of an eventual settlement with Britain. These conservatives, many of whom were Southerners, thought that reunion could be better achieved by war than by negotiation. 'Let us beat them into compliance,' a Virginian wrote; 'they will be glad to receive us on those terms [acknowledgement of the colonies' legislative autonomy], rather than lose us altogether.'[1] Enthusiastic in rebellion, the Southerners still had no intention of sanctioning revolution. 'We do not want to be independent,' wrote Joseph Hewes of North Carolina in

[1] 4 *Am. Arch.* v. 1159.

the summer of 1775, 'we want no revolution, unless a change of Ministry and measures would be deemed such. We are loyal subjects of our present most gracious Sovereign.'[2]

Most of the Whig leaders outside New England seemed to regard war with Britain, not as a means to independence, but as an alternative to, even as security against, revolution. The war, they saw, gave a temporary unity of purpose to all Americans except outright Tories, and also directed against the British energies that might otherwise turn against the established social order in the colonies. The Rutledges in South Carolina, Hewes and William Hooper in North Carolina, Benjamin Harrison and Edmund Pendleton in Virginia, Thomas Johnson and Samuel Chase in Maryland, Dickinson and James Wilson in Pennsylvania, and Jay and Duane in New York, all, whether intentionally or not, were trying to turn the wrath of the times away from themselves by allowing it freely to assault Britain. Yet these men fiercely resisted outright independence with its alarming opportunities for constitutional change. Their hope was to be able, victorious in arms, to negotiate with Britain for a restoration of the old negligent connexion so rudely disturbed by British policies after 1763. If this could be done, then the nominal sovereignty of Britain might again shelter the existing provincial oligarchies.

John Dickinson was foremost among those who held to a desperate hope of reconciliation. He thought the Association should be carried out 'with tenderness, so as to convince our brethren in Great Britain of the importance of a connection and harmony between them and us'. The interests of Britain and America were still the same; independence was not only inherently undesirable, but would be 'dear bought and at best . . . frequently convulsed and precarious'. In May 1775

---

[2] Ibid. ii. 1757. Tories found it dangerous to intimate that the Congress intended to declare American independence. On 4 Aug. 1775, for example, the New York Committee declared a man to be 'an enemy to this country' for having predicted independence by the following March. Ibid. iii. 21.

Dickinson and James Duane persuaded the Congress to put the colonies into a state of defence, and at the same time to present 'an humble and dutiful petition' to the King. The Congress also accepted a clause, written by Duane, resolving to bring about a negotiation in order to 'accommodate the unhappy disputes'. Even the Tories caught a glimmer of hope in this.[3]

The New Englanders almost lost their composure. John Adams wrote that the business of preparing war and talking conciliation at the same time gave a 'whimsical Cast' to the proceedings of the Congress. 'We must have a Petition to the King,' he wrote, 'and a delicate Proposal of Negociation, etc. This Negociation I dread like Death: But it must be proposed. We can't avoid it. Discord and total Disunion would be the certain Effect of a resolute Refusal to petition and negociate.' When Dickinson's petition was being considered, Adams spoke against it with some heat, however, and Dickinson afterwards accosted him in the State House yard and asked 'in a most abrupt and extraordinary manner': 'What is the reason, Mr. Adams, that you New-Englandmen oppose our measures of reconciliation? . . . Look ye! If you don't concur with us in our pacific system, I and a number of us will break off from you in New England, and we will carry on the opposition by ourselves in our own way.' Adams wrote bitterly of Dickinson, that 'a certain great Fortune and piddling Genius . . . has given a silly Cast to our whole Doings'.[4]

In July 1775 the Congress adopted Dickinson's petition to the King, expressing a continuing desire by the colonies for a connexion with Britain. 'Let this be ever considered as a family quarrel,' Dickinson wrote, 'disgraceful and *ruinous* into which we are innocently plunged by intolerable oppression, and which we are sincerely disposed to appease and

---

[3] *Journals of the Continental Congress*, ii. 61, 65; Miller, *American Revolution*, pp. 420–1.

[4] *Letters of Members of the Continental Congress*, i. 152; Adams, *Works*, ii. 410.

reconcile.'[5] A sceptic might have reassured the New Englanders by pointing out that even family quarrels are rarely reconciled when one party has such a firm conviction of injured innocence.

Through the winter of 1775–6 the conservatives were strong enough to block any overt move towards independence, and the New Englanders had to be content with specific measures for carrying on the war. These, it is true, drew the colonies further into the hurry of action and further away from discussion. Nevertheless, the Southerners, with few exceptions, continued to hope for reconciliation. Thomas Johnson of Maryland, for example, wrote that there were two aims to the war, the first to establish American liberties, the second to achieve a reunion with Britain, 'so may we preserve the empire entire, and the constitutional liberty, founded in whiggish principles, handed down to us by our ancestors.' America, he thought, should avoid all constitutional innovation so as to keep herself united and Britain divided. This would eventually gain the colonies the support of 'every honest Englishman', and enable the good English Whigs to overthrow the 'cunning Scotchmen' in the Ministry.[6]

Gradually, however, anti-New-England sentiment grew among the other delegates to the Congress as they realized how far towards independence they had gone, and how difficult it would be to turn back. They began to refer petulantly to Boston as 'the Zealous City', and call the New Englanders 'wise men of the East'. As the months passed and they failed to get any encouragement from Britain, the conservatives found that in opposing independence they were trying to brake the momentum of the cart they had themselves helped push over the top of the hill. They were slow to see that there was nothing to do but hang on or jump out. Early in January 1776 James Wilson of Pennsylvania tried to stop the progression towards independence. He brought in a motion strongly

---

[5] Alexander, *A Revolutionary Conservative*, p. 113.
[6] *Letters of Members of the Continental Congress*, i. 190.

supported by the delegates from the Middle Colonies asking the Congress to declare its intentions as to independence. Since an outright declaration of independence could not yet be carried, the New Englanders were alarmed. John Adams wrote that they were 'between Hawk and Buzzard'. They had to allow Wilson to draw up his proposed address to the constituents of the Congress. It was 'very long, badly written, and full against Independency', and to the delight of the New Englanders, the Congress rejected it.[7]

It was at this moment that Tom Paine, with superb timing, published his *Common Sense*. Taken out of its context of revolution, *Common Sense* is not entirely convincing. Paine's anarchist justification for revolution was arguable, as was his assumption that the only alternative to total American independence was total submission to Britain. Yet the impact of *Common Sense*, as it went through one printing after another, was enormous, measurably affecting men who, at any other time, very likely would have found Paine's philosophical beliefs hateful and his political argument superficial. Charles Lee, for example, wrote to George Washington that he had been convinced of the necessity of separation from England by Paine's pamphlet. Washington himself wrote that the 'sound doctrine and unanswerable reasoning' of *Common Sense* was working a 'powerful change . . . in the minds of men'. A New Yorker wrote that 'a pamphlet entitled "Common Sense" has converted thousands to Independence, that could not endure the idea before'. A Philadelphian wrote, 'as many as read, so many become converted, though perhaps the hour before [they] were most violent against the least idea of Independence'.[8] All of which suggests how necessary it was, especially for a scriptural-minded people, to find *Common Sense* in theory for what had been for many months common sense in practice.

[7] *Letters of Members of the Continental Congress*, i. 301, 304; Jensen, *Articles of Confederation*, pp. 88–89.
[8] Tyler, *Literary History*, i. 468–73.

As a final gesture in pursuance of the Anglican Tories' compact to 'watch and confute all publications that threatened mischief', Charles Inglis duly wrote a reply to *Common Sense*. His *True Interest of America*, however, would not have brought back out of rebellion very many who had been convinced by Paine, although at another time, its arguments might have seemed quite reasonable. In any case, the facilities that had enabled more than a hundred thousand copies of *Common Sense* to be printed were not available to print replies to it. The times were growing too warm for public argument, and the few hundred copies of his pamphlet that Inglis had managed to get printed in New York were taken out of his printer's house and burnt on the Common by a mob.[9]

If many conservative Whigs were persuaded by *Common Sense* and the march of events to accept American independence, there were a few who held out. To the general surprise and occasional amusement of the Tories, there began to come over to the Loyalist camp little groups of dissident Whigs. Some were thoughtful and scrupulous men; others were opportunistic, frightened, or merely stubborn. Numerically, the Whig Loyalists were never to be important; they hold a certain interest, however, for their point of view.

One of the thoughtful and scrupulous of these late Loyalists was Peter Van Schaack of New York. Van Schaack had apparently supported the revolutionary movement wholeheartedly until 1775. He was a rationalist and an individualist, concerned to keep his political principles 'strictly agreeable to those of Mr. Locke'. He was indifferent to the traditions the Tories cherished, and to him the apprehensions of men like Inglis and Chandler were obscure and antique. His very individualism, however, led Van Schaack to question the new unanimity rising out of the Revolution. He began to resist the pressures towards unthinking conformity that were making

[9] Tyler, *Literary History*, i. 480–1; Lydekker, *Life of Inglis*, pp. 149–52. Inglis's pamphlet was published some months later in Philadelphia. For a discussion of his argument with Paine, see below, pp. 184–6.

compliant revolutionists of men far less liberal than himself.
His own political speculations were unhurried and cool, and
with deliberation he turned his back on the rush of events in
order to consult his reason and his conscience, for the consistency of his own conduct, he wrote, 'however insignificant to
others, is to me of the utmost importance'. During the winter of
1775–6, when friends like Gouverneur Morris and John Jay had
put aside thought and were busy with war, Van Schaack shut
himself up at his farm with his books. He went through and
annotated Locke, Vattel, Montesquieu, Grotius, Beccaria, and
Puffendorf, and then wrote out his opinions on the Revolution.

Van Schaack began by accepting the right of revolution.
He thought that the doctrine of passive obedience which
denied an oppressed people a right to revolt was an argument
for slavery. 'But my difficulty', he wrote of the troubles with
Britain, 'arises from this, that taking the whole of the acts
complained of together, they do not, I think, manifest a
system of slavery, but may fairly be imputed to human frailty,
and the difficulty of the subject.' Perhaps, he decided, the
British were misguided rather than wicked: 'In short, I think
those acts may have been passed without a preconcerted plan
of enslaving us.'

Having once allowed that there might not be a plot to
enslave America, it was perfectly simple for Van Schaack to
make Loyalists of himself and John Locke. For without insup-
portable tyranny, society could not be dissolved, a state of
nature did not exist, and a man could not take up arms against
the government. He had supported the Congress, Van Schaack
wrote, until he had decided it was aiming at a dissolution of
the union between Britain and America. That, he could not
support, nor could he be bound by the opinion of any majority.
He realized, he wrote diffidently, that many men 'of the
soundest integrity' had taken up arms against Britain. 'But',
he concluded, 'this is too serious a matter, implicitly to yield
to the authority of any character, however respectable. Every
man must exercise his own reason, and judge for himself.'

Following his conclusion, Van Schaack wrote that, 'Whatever disagreeable consequences may follow from dissenting from the general voice', no man would be justified in taking part in measures which he believed might cause unnecessary distress and suffering to his fellow men. He quoted Locke, 'For he that appeals to Heaven, must be sure that he has right on his side.' If criticized for his stand, Van Schaack wrote that he would ask, 'who has constituted you the judge of the rule of right for me, and what claim have you to infallibility? . . . Do you not differ in opinion as much from me as I do from you, and have I not as much right to blame you as you have me for this difference?'

In claiming absolutely the 'sacred right of private judgment', Van Schaack brought Locke to bear on the Revolution in a way that had not occurred to the revolutionists. For even if there had been tyranny enough to dissolve the old allegiance (which Van Schaack denied), then each man had a right to contract his own new allegiance. He could not be subjected to a new government without his consent, for that would deprive him of the protection of the laws he had had under the old régime, without offering him anything in its place except coercion. If the new government compelled the allegiance of the Loyalists, or punished them for not giving up the old allegiance, where, Van Schaack asked, were 'the sacred rights of mankind' which formed the Revolution's own justification? Thus did Van Schaack, seriously, but perhaps also with a touch of irony, destroy one of the principal logical foundations of the Revolution.[10]

At first sight Councillor William Smith seems another New York Whig who belatedly joined the Loyalists. There appears to be some doubt, however, that Smith, although he was certainly a late Loyalist, was ever a Whig at all, except in local affairs. It is true that he was one of the founders of the Whig Club in New York and, according to Colden, had been a

[10] H. C. Van Schaack, *Life of Peter Van Schaack* (New York, 1842), pp. 54–60, 73–76, 87, 260–1.

'principal adviser' to the faction in opposition to the royal government. In 1770 Colden had written that 'Mr Smith takes a pleasure in throwing the Administration into disorder', and as late as 1774 he was still regarded unsuspiciously by the revolutionists. Yet Smith, although he did not know Galloway and regarded Hutchinson as 'a mere scribbling Governor', seems to have stood somewhere between these men in his view of America's relations with Britain.

Like so many New Yorkers, Smith was both cosmopolitan and provincial, narrowly concerned, on the one hand, with the petty intrigues and family feuds of his province, but, at the same time, intellectually at home in an Anglo-American world much wider than that in which most Americans lived. His Whiggish commitments were in the small theatre of New York politics, where family tradition had placed him in the outer circle of the local oligarchy. His discontent with the royal government was more like Galloway's, however, than like Dickinson's or John Adams's, in that he lamented its weakness, not its strength. 'Would to God we had a little more Government here', he had written early in the dispute with Britain.

Although he was not a delegate, Smith hoped the First Continental Congress would negotiate a settlement with Britain, and was disappointed with its actual proceedings. He refused to sign the Association and took no part in organizing the Provincial Congress. In December 1775 he suggested a plan of reconciliation to the Provincial Congress, which he hoped to associate with the New Jersey Assembly's proposed petition to the King. The Congress refused to consider his plan, however, and when the New Jersey Assembly dropped its petition, Smith retired up the Hudson to his farm. There he maintained an uneasy neutrality, carrying on relations both with the British and with his old Whig friends, until finally, in the middle of the war, he joined the Loyalists in New York.[11]

[11] *N.Y. Col. Doc.* viii. 62, 221, 257, 653–4; 4 *Am. Arch.* iv. 394, 406–7; Smith, *Historical Memoirs*, pp. 39, 190–2, 252–3. Smith's plan of concilia-

Neutrality rather than Loyalism was the characteristic refuge of the conservative Whigs in New York. By the end of 1775 none of the revolutionary committees in New York, except the ungentlemanly Committee of Mechanicks, could muster anything like its full membership. Not only was the Provincial Congress unable to persuade delegates from more than five out of the twelve counties to attend, but the president of the Congress, P. V. B. Livingston, had retired up-river and refused to return, pleading illness. The Committee of Safety had difficulty persuading its members to attend meetings: one man was ill and could not wear his shoes; another had an itch; another's wife was ill. The Committee had 120 members, but in order to meet at all, had to reduce its quorum from 33 to 27, and finally to 21.[12]

The convinced revolutionists would not admit that the original resistance to Britain had changed its character, and accused their conservative brethren of inconstancy. A New York pamphleteer wrote that 'the very men who have now luckily fallen into such a pleasant dream of loyalty and obedience, in the time of the Stamp Act, were most of them "patriots of distinguished note"; the most vociferous clamorers for liberty and property; the life and soul of mobs . . . They then thought it no treason, no mortal sin, no Republican or Presbyterian contrivance, to form a Continental Congress'.[13] The dissident Whigs replied that the Stamp Act Congress had contented itself with protesting against the Stamp Act, and

tion included a proposed new constitution, apparently modelled on the Albany Plan of 1754, whereby there would have been a general American legislature of two houses, an elected House of Deputies and an appointed Council, presided over by a lord lieutenant, 'as in Ireland'. Smith's legislature, unlike that proposed by Galloway, would have had only taxing powers—and even there would have left the actual assessment and collection of taxes to the separate provinces. See Smith, *History of New York*, i., pp. xi–xiii.

For Smith's later career as Chief Justice of Quebec, see Hilda Neatby, 'Chief Justice William Smith: An Eighteenth Century Whig Imperialist', *Canadian Historical Review*, xxviii. 44–67.

[12] 4 *Am. Arch.* iii. 1751 ff.; Becker, *Political Parties*, pp. 226–7, 234–6.
[13] 4 *Am. Arch.* iii. 1735.

had not set itself up as a new government for America as the Continental Congress had done.

In Philadelphia the best statement of the case of the doubtful Whigs was made by the Reverend William Smith, who, after having deserted Boucher and the New York clergy in order to support the Congress, now had a change of heart. Smith was a clever, bibulous Scot, who, according to John Adams, was 'looking up to government for a pair of lawn sleeves'. Adams called him 'one of the many irregular and extravagant characters of the age', but complimented him on his abilities, 'which are generally allowed to be good'.[14]

Smith seems to have hoped he could work amicably with the revolutionists, as he had done for so many years with the local Presbyterians. Even so, although he had little regard for the High Churchmen of New York, he was a bad rebel. Early in 1776 he wrote a pamphlet, *Plain Truth*, in answer to *Common Sense*; he also wrote a number of articles against independence, signed 'Cato'. From a philosophical point of view *Plain Truth* was a confused and compromised answer to Paine, which suffers by comparison with the lucid and forthright conservatism of Inglis's *The True Interest of America*. Smith's observations do illuminate, however, the unhappy position of the conservative Whigs.

'If we look back to the origin of the present controversy', Smith wrote, 'it will appear that some among us ... have been constantly enlarging their views, and stretching them beyond their first bounds, till at length they have wholly changed their ground.' Smith recalled that the dispute with Britain had originally concerned the question of parliamentary taxation, not American independence. Although, he wrote, it was well known that some men had aimed at independence from the beginning, it had been 'reckoned slanderous, inimical to America, and what not, to intimate the least suspicion of this kind'. Now, despite all the resolves and instructions of their constituents abhorring independence, the radicals in the Con-

---

[14] Adams, *Works*, ii. 358, 360, 362; 4 *Am. Arch.* iv. 1562.

gress were pretending to be driven to separation from Britain. The radical leaders, according to Smith, were not even sincere republicans, but only adventurers using the people as a ladder to power. Smith then cited much textual evidence from Locke and Montesquieu, as well as from the Bible, Plato, Tacitus, and Polybius, in order to prove that democrats and demagogues were enemies of true liberty.

The least the Congress could do, Smith wrote, was to consult the people before making a 'leap in the dark' into independence. They would apparently prefer, however, to declare independence on the advice of the committees and conventions alone: 'thus we may be echoed and re-echoed out of our liberties, our property, our happiness, and plunged deeper and deeper into . . . war and bloodshed, without ever being consulted'. It was nonsense, Smith wrote, to maintain as Paine had done, that the outbreak of war had made negotiation or reconciliation impossible, for all wars aimed at peace. There could be no harm in negotiating with Britain, for America could always reject unacceptable terms, and be in a stronger position than if no discussion were admitted. Smith pointed out that the colonies had already demonstrated their practical independence, and this he regarded, not as an argument for final separation, but as reason for a safe and honourable return to a connexion with Britain. If the proposed British peace commissioners made a decent offer, he wrote, 'my voice shall be for an immediate reconciliation'. Smith revealed the disagreeable plight of the conservative Whigs, however, when he admitted ruefully that, 'when the last necessity comes, I have no expedient in view but to take my chance with you [i.e. with the Congress] for better and for worse'. Characteristically, Smith never became an overt Loyalist.[15]

In Philadelphia, especially, the revolutionary movement was acquiring articulate democratic aims, and this produced

[15] William Smith [pseud. 'Candidus'], *Plain Truth . . . etc.* (London, 1776); id., 'Letters of Cato', 4 *Am. Arch.* v. 126–7, 188–90, 443–6, 514–17, 542–6 839–43, 850–3, 1049–51.

the most widespread and least creditable outbreak of pruden-
tial loyalty to Britain in the colonies. Some of the radical
thrusts at these late Loyalists struck home, like that of the
Philadelphian who wrote, 'They tell you, "they had rather be
governed by the mild and wise laws of Great Britain, than the
decrees of an American mob." The truth is, neither they, nor
their principals, wish to be governed by any laws that will
effectually secure the liberty and property of the people from
their ravenous clutches.'[16]

The first serious trouble in the Whig ranks of Philadelphia
came during the summer of 1775 when a number of radicals
decided that a notorious Tory 'ought to receive an American
coat of tar and feathers', for having tried to get a summons
issued against a committee member. The man was seized, but
the radicals 'met with such opposition from some who ought
to have stood foremost in support of the Committee', that they
let him go. One of the committeemen who had planned the
affair wrote indignantly: 'we are exceedingly surprised at the
conduct of some gentlemen on the occasion, especially of him
who threatened to . . . have four of us whipped at the cart's
tail, and of him also who laboured so indefatigably to bring
a battalion to fire upon us. . . . The freemen of this County
would have those gentlemen, who value themselves so highly
on their wealth and possessions to know that they do not
esteem it the sole end of Government to protect the rich and
the powerful.'[17]

The class conflict in Philadelphia broke the revolutionary
movement there in two. The conservatives began to hope for
a reconciliation with Britain as a means of regaining control
locally, and the radicals were forced to abandon the pretence
that theirs was a liberal movement. In September 1775 the
Philadelphia Committee decided that liberty of dissent had
become a dispensable luxury. A resolution of the Committee
admitted the right of free speech, except when used 'for the
purpose of raising jealousies among the people, distracting

[16] 4 *Am. Arch.* v. 87.   [17] Ibid. iii. 170–6.

their counsels, and counteracting their virtuous exertions against injury and oppression'. In such a case 'all laws, human and divine, justify the punishment of such licentiousness'. The Committee thereupon adopted the tyrant's usual plea of necessity: 'no person has a right to the protection of a community or society he wishes to destroy'.[18]

James Allen was typical of the disillusioned Pennsylvania Whigs. In July 1775 he began to worry about the difficulty of restoring order after victory over Britain, but then he reminded himself, 'It is a great & glorious cause. The Eyes of Europe are upon us.' By October his enthusiasm had sensibly diminished. He had, it is true, joined a militia company: 'My Inducement principally to join them is: that a man is suspected who does not . . . & I believe discreet people mixing with them, may keep them in Order. . . . With all my zeal for the great cause . . . I frequently cry out—Dreadful times!' By March 1776 Allen was despondent: 'The plot thickens;' he wrote, 'peace is scarcely thought of—Independency predominant. Thinking people uneasy, irresolute & inactive . . . I love the Cause of liberty; but cannot heartily join in the prosecution of measures totally foreign to the original plan of Resistance. The madness of the multitude is but one degree better than submission to the Tea-Act.' Allen was also typical of the disappointed Whigs in that he never became an outright Loyalist.[19]

In the spring of 1776 a Philadelphian who had been a Loyalist all along wrote with some amusement that 'the saints of this place are, many of them, turned sinners'. The town was disfigured by a veritable rash of pamphlets and articles opposing independence, written by Whigs, not Tories. A man who called himself 'Rationalis' wrote a diatribe against republics and fumed against the 'tyranny of [the] many'. A 'Settled Citizen', contemplating the advance of democracy in Pennsylvania, suddenly thought he saw in the English, 'some traces

[18] Ibid. 731.
[19] 'Diary of James Allen', *Pennsylvania Magazine of History and Biography*, ix. 184–6.

of that nobility of sentiment and action which were formerly characteristick of the British nation'.[20]

A Philadelphian who called himself 'Civis' wrote a number of articles opposing independence which expressed clearly the indignation the old Whigs felt at the new men who had taken over their cause. 'Civis' was loath to 'explore the dark and untrodden way of Independence and Republicanism'. He railed against 'these innovators', and wrote that a great proportion of the Philadelphia radicals were minors, apprentices, and immigrants. He pleaded that the old Pennsylvania constitution should not be thrown aside 'to let in the ambitious, Republican schemes of a set of men whom nobody knows'. He denied scornfully that those who opposed independence were Tories. 'The opposers of Independence', he wrote, 'are the true Whigs, who are for preserving the Constitution, as well against the secret machinations of ambitious innovators as against the open attacks of the British Parliament; they are the men who first set on foot the present opposition, and who, I trust, will, if they are permitted to go on, bring it to a happy conclusion.' What 'Civis' meant was that he and his friends were believers in the divine right of oligarchy, men who had reviled Galloway for wanting the British to have a greater share in managing Pennsylvania's affairs, and who now were equally astonished at the idea of men 'whom nobody knows' wanting to help govern the province.[21]

The people whom a local radical called 'the family compact' of Pennsylvania were worried. Colonel Joseph Reed wrote to Robert Morris that he had never opposed reconciliation, provided British taxation was given up, and control over local affairs given to Americans; he saw no reason why a reunion might not be achieved on those terms. For his part, Morris wrote, 'Where the plague are these Commissioners, if they are to come what is it that detains them?'[22]

[20] 4 *Am. Arch.* iv. 1153, 1527–30; v. 1036–8.   [21] Ibid. 802–4, 1140–3.
[22] 5 *Am. Arch.* i. 415; *Letters of Members of the Continental Congress,* i. 416.

The British, however, did nothing to help the oligarchs out of their difficulties.

It was in Pennsylvania, where the threat of democracy was most pressing, that the fever of late loyalty burned highest. But in all the colonies outside New England distinguished Whigs were having second thoughts about the Revolution. In Maryland Daniel Dulany, after having eloquently opposed parliamentary taxation, had refused to acknowledge the authority of the Congress, and had left the province; but Charles Carroll and Daniel of St. Thomas Jenifer were still working for a reconciliation with Britain and keeping on terms with the Congress at the same time. In May 1776 the Maryland Convention advised the Maryland delegates to the Continental Congress that they still hoped for a reconciliation and that they would support the struggle 'on the principles of the Union as explained at the time of entering on the War'. When the Congress urged the Maryland Council of Safety to seize the royal governor, Thomas Eden, the Council declared that the Congress was trying to make itself dictator of the continent. Eden was allowed to leave the colony without molestation, and the Council of Safety even expressed to him 'their real wishes for your return to resume the Government of this Province'.[23]

A Virginian who called himself 'Hampden' wrote that a 'constitutional Independence', by which he meant freedom from British taxation, should have been the American object from the beginning, but that the 'necessity of a total separation from Britain does not yet arise'. He praised the British constitution and wrote that the 're-establishment of our original . . . Independency' would be sufficient. Britain was, after all, an 'outwork of defence' for Americans against the ambitions of Europe, and was also a useful arbiter of disputes among the colonies themselves. Besides, 'Hampden' thought, the seat of empire would eventually be transferred to America,

[23] Ibid. 464; 4 *Am. Arch.* v. 1594–6; Miller, *American Revolution*, pp. 489–90.

so that independence might lose Britain to America, rather than the other way round.[24]

Carter Braxton wrote to Landon Carter that he was more afraid of France than of Britain. He had decided the New Englanders had given up all thought of reconciliation and wanted merely to 'embrace their darling Democracy'. A number of Virginia conservatives, led by Edmund Pendleton and Benjamin Harrison, considered negotiating separately with the British through the royal governor, Lord Drummond.[25]

Two of the principal Whig leaders in North Carolina, Joseph Hewes and James Iredell, were vigorously opposed to independence, and Iredell wrote a pamphlet in June 1776 in which he pleaded that a connexion with Britain, 'in spite of every provocation, would be the happier for America, for a considerable time to come, than *absolute independence*'. John and Edward Rutledge, the South Carolina Whig leaders, had tried to resign from the Continental Congress early in 1776. Edward Rutledge wrote in June 1776 that he was afraid independence would subject all the colonies to New England control: 'The Force of their Arms I hold exceeding Cheap', he wrote bombastically, 'but I confess I dread their overruling Influence in Council. I dread their low Cunning, and . . . levelling Principles.' Rutledge added naïvely that he and his friends wished to 'keep the Staff in our own hands'.[26]

It is a relief to turn from the calculating loyalty of the conservative Whigs to the forthrightness of the New Englanders, who by the spring of 1776 no longer bothered to conceal their contempt for those of their fellow revolutionists who opposed independence. John Adams wrote scornfully, 'Independency is a Hobgoblin of so frightful Mien, that it would throw a delicate Person into Fits to look it in the Face.' Joseph Hawley wrote to a fellow Massachusetts man, 'For *God's* sake let there

[24] 4 *Am. Arch.* v. 1157–60.
[25] *Letters of Members of the Continental Congress*, i. 368, 420–1; Adams, *Works*, iii. 31.
[26] Jensen, *Articles of Confederation*, pp. 26–29; 4 *Am. Arch.* v. 572; *Letters of Members of the Continental Congress*, i. 476–7, 517–18.

be a Full Revolution, or all has been done in vain. Independency, and a well planned Continental Government, will save us.'

The New Englanders at the Congress had waited patiently until a year of waging war and almost two years of making legislation had accustomed their colleagues to the reality of independence. They listened to a last outpouring of sentiment about the connexion with Britain, and then nudged the Southerners into accepting a declaration of independence which, from New England's point of view, was obligingly written by a useful Virginian. Some of the conservatives made this easy by absenting themselves from the Congress, like Robert Morris and John Dickinson of Pennsylvania, and all the New Yorkers. Others put their consciences at ease by throwing up their hands and saying, like Joseph Hewes of North Carolina, 'It is done! and I will abide by it.'[27]

The Declaration of Independence made a good many neutrals, but it did not make many outright Loyalists. The true Whigs did not become Loyalists because it would not have paid. They were practical men whose chief interest was 'to keep the Staff' in their own hands, or if they let it slip, to wait and watch until they could pick it up. To lose position and property rather than make their peace with the course of events did not appeal to them. It was more sensible to do as James Duane did, to become a careful neutral and look forward to the 'rich Encrease of our Estates', which would assuredly follow in the wake of free trade with the world.[28] It was not oligarchs as such who became Loyalists, but only the weakest or least practical oligarchs.

[27] *Letters of Members of the Continental Congress*, i. 405–6, 537; 4 *Am. Arch.* v. 1168–9.
[28] Alexander, *A Revolutionary Conservative*, p. 120.

CHAPTER VII

Disenchantment

By the summer of 1776, when the Declaration of Independence was adopted, the Loyalists were nowhere sufficiently strong in organization or confidence to act on their own initiative. Where they had attempted to rise, they had been suppressed; elsewhere they were intimidated. Their hopes now lay entirely with the British. Despite British reverses in New England, most of the Loyalists seem still to have expected a swift restoration of the royal government's authority, at least in the Middle and Southern Colonies. They were elated when Sir William Howe's army was debarked on Staten Island, and, after the first British victories on Long Island, hopeful of the imminent collapse of the forces of revolution.

British policy, however, had entrusted to Lord Howe and his brother not only the command of military forces sufficient to destroy the Continental Army, but also a commission to negotiate for a peaceful submission of the rebels. Of this dual commission, to wage war and to make peace, the Howes were at first more serious in attempting the latter. Never, apparently, until he was removed from his command in 1778, did Sir William Howe entirely abandon hope of finding a political rather than a military solution to the problems of the Revolution. To the Loyalists this appeasement of rebellion was crime and folly. As early as June 1776 Boucher wrote that he expected only bad news from America, since the King's commanders were 'antiministerialist and wish for ill-success'.[1] The Loyalists were convinced that nothing but the destruction of Washington's forces could discourage the revolutionists. 'But', as Thomas Jones, the Tory historian of New York, afterwards

[1] Boucher, 'Letters', viii. 60; ix. 236.

wrote, 'a different set of politics at this time prevailed, the rebels were to be converted, the loyalists frowned upon. Proclamations were to end an inveterate rebellion.'[2]

After the British failure to destroy Washington's army in the fighting around New York, the Tories' criticism of the Howes became vehement. It seemed that again and again the Howes, either deliberately or with unbelievable negligence, allowed Washington's army to escape annihilation. Why, the Loyalists asked, had Lord Howe not sent his fleet up the East River to prevent the escape of the Americans from Long Island? 'But this was not done,' Jones wrote, 'and why it was not, let the brothers Howe tell.' Again, Jones thought that Sir William Howe could have destroyed the American forces at White Plains. When a captured American general told Jones that Providence had put a mist before Howe's eyes, Jones commented that the Americans were more obliged to the English opposition than to Providence.[3]

The Loyalists criticized General Howe unmercifully for his conduct of the campaign in New Jersey. Instead of keeping after Washington, Jones wrote, 'A victorious army, in full pursuit of a flying inconsiderable enemy' was halted and permitted to plunder friendly civilians. Galloway maintained that Howe could easily have overtaken Washington, and observed that even though he had made an unnecessary delay, he had still arrived at Trenton before Washington's last boat was across the Delaware. He thought Howe had deliberately allowed Washington to escape into Pennsylvania, and told Governor Hutchinson later that 'there was never a week' when Howe could not have destroyed the Continental Army had he wanted to.[4]

In the autumn of 1776 the Philadelphia Loyalists expected the British to enter that city almost at any day. Galloway

---

[2] Jones, *History*, i. 121.

[3] Ibid. 114, 124; *Winslow Papers*, pp. 36–37.

[4] Jones, *History*, i. 126–7; Galloway, *Examination . . . before the House of Commons*, pp. 39–43; id., *Letters to a Nobleman on the Conduct of the War* (London, 1780), pp. 50–51; Hutchinson, *Diary*, ii. 247.

observed that the Pennsylvania militia could not be roused to oppose Howe in New Jersey, and he doubted that Washington could have raised another force had the British scattered his troops and advanced on Philadelphia. He pointed out that the Continental Congress was sufficiently in a state of panic at this time to allow Philadelphia to negotiate with Howe for its safety. He wrote, however, that the defeat of the Hessians at Trenton, which he blamed on Howe's faulty disposition of his troops, had a 'very mischievous effect to the British service', since it revived the spirits of the Continental Army and prompted the Pennsylvania militia to turn out.[5]

The Loyalists' criticism of Howe's campaign in 1776 was mild compared with their opinion of his measures the following year. Galloway thought that the proper strategy in 1777 should have been an attack on the New England coast made in conjunction with Burgoyne's descent from Canada.[6] If, however, Philadelphia was to be the object of Howe's advance, why, Galloway asked, did he not come by land, or by an expedition up the Delaware? 'Why', he wrote, 'was so high-spirited an army taken from the sight of an enemy of not half its force', and sent six hundred miles by sea to get sixty miles by land?[7] Boucher wrote that there was no reason whatever

[5] Galloway, *Examination . . . before the House of Commons*, p. 17; 'Diary of James Allen', p. 190. Galloway's views on the state of opinion in the Middle Colonies is supported by Washington's observations, made in a letter to his brother, dated 18 Dec. 1776: 'Between you and me I think our Affairs are in a very bad situation; not so much from the apprehension of Genl. Howe's Army, as from the defection of New York, Jerseys, and Pennsylvania. In short, the Conduct of the Jerseys has been most Infamous. Instead of turning out to defend their Country and affording aid to our Army, they are making their submissions as fast as they can.' George Washington, *Writings from the Original Manuscript Sources*, ed. J. C. Fitzpatrick (33 vols., Washington, 1931–41), vi. 397–8.

[6] Jones, on the other hand, described the garrisoning of Newport, Rhode Island, as a 'Don Quixote expedition' which wasted 10,000 men and 100 ships that might have been used in the campaign to take Philadelphia. *History*, i. 130–1.

[7] Galloway, *Letters to a Nobleman*, pp. 46, 68–72; *Examination . . . before the House of Commons*, pp. 26–35; *Reply to the Observations of Lieut. Gen. Sir Wm. Howe* (London, 1780), pp. 45 ff., 72–111.

for the 'monstrously tedious & expensive Voyage' down to and
up Chesapeake Bay, an expedition which Jonathan Sewell
described succinctly as follows: 'away they come—down the
river again—huzza—make a circle round Asspeak, up Chesapeake, and after travelling in the heat of the season, in a hell
of a climate, over a monstrous extent of country, they arrive
at Philadelphia—*"the army in high spirits"*'.[8]

The Loyalists thought that the Chesapeake manœuvre,
apart from its inherent unsoundness, contributed to Burgoyne's defeat. They did not accuse Howe, as some later
writers did, of refusing to co-operate with Burgoyne, but they
did maintain that he was negligent of his duty in placing his
army in a position where he could give no aid to Burgoyne.
Most of all, however, the Loyalists blamed Howe for having
failed to dispose of Washington's army before the disaster at
Saratoga. They regarded not only the Chesapeake expedition,
but Howe's strategy during the whole year's campaign, and
even his tactics on the field, as evidence of his unwillingness
to destroy the Continental Army.

'The Conduct of Gen[l] Howe is unaccountable', James Allen
wrote in September 1777, 'nor do we conceive what is his
object. . . . In the Spring he might have done any thing;
the Whigs are in great spirits.' Galloway accused Howe of
regularly declining to exploit his victories, observing that after
all the major engagements in the Middle Colonies, from Long
Island and White Plains to Brandywine and Germantown,
Washington, although defeated, had been allowed a respite to
re-form his scattered forces. 'Neither of the generals . . . [had]
any keen appetite for fighting,' Galloway wrote of Washington
and Howe after Germantown, '. . . one, because he knew he
could not conquer, and the other, because he feared he should
conquer too soon.'[9]

---

[8] Boucher, 'Letters', ix. 335; Curwen, *Journal*, p. 207.
[9] 'Diary of James Allen', p. 288; Galloway, *Examination . . . before the
House of Commons*, p. 70; id., *Reply to Howe*, pp. 34–35, 39–44; id., *Letters
to a Nobleman*, pp. 47, 74, 86.

'It is truly an irksome and painful task, for a liberal mind', Galloway wrote, 'to travel through all the misconduct of this campaign.' Not even Galloway, however, who was perhaps his most stringent critic, ascribed General Howe's failures to incompetence; 'he succeeded', Galloway wrote, 'as far as he chose'. Nor did he find fault with the Howes for pursuing political, as well as military ends. 'Every man', he wrote, 'who wishes to reduce a country will make the minds and disposi- tions of the people the first great objects of his attention; and these are often more easily gained by policy than force.' What Galloway, in common with most of the other Loyalists, ob- jected to was that the Howes pursued the wrong political ends. Galloway wrote that Lord Howe made no attempt to exploit the disunion of the colonies, and tried to deal only with those Americans who would, under no circumstances, deal with him, while to the 'well-affected' he was 'equivocal, obscure, and secret'.[10]

Almost all the Loyalists who recorded their opinions com- plained that the British neglected them. One of their most frequent accusations was that, during the first part of the war, the British would not embody Loyalist volunteers. Edward Winslow, for example, commented bitterly on General Howe's refusal to arm and equip a small group of Tories who called themselves the 'New York Volunteers': 'It was not credited', he wrote, 'that a General whose command was so extensive could possibly want the power to furnish common necessaries for 200 men, if his disposition toward them was favorable.'[11]

The British, for their part, had their own reasons for dis- trusting the Loyalists. In New England in the first stages of the war they had found themselves among an indisputably hostile population, with the local Tories a mere handful of frightened refugees. This had undoubtedly coloured their

[10] Galloway, *A Letter to the Right Honourable Lord Viscount H—e* (London, 1781), pp. 3, 4, 5, 9; id., *Letters to a Nobleman*, pp. 29–31, 68.

[11] *Winslow Papers*, pp. 43–44; see also Galloway, *Reply to Howe*, pp. 19–20; id., *Letter to Howe*, pp. 35–42; Allen, 'Diary', p. 438; C. H. Van Tyne, *The Loyalists in the American Revolution* (New York, 1902), p. 246.

views of Loyalist strength, and they were slow to realize the quite different circumstances of the Tories in the Middle Colonies. They seem not to have appreciated the numerical strength of the New York and Pennsylvania Loyalists, but only to have observed the feebleness of Loyalist organization and activity. That this feebleness was real can hardly be questioned. Lord Howe was not entirely a victim of his Whig prejudices when he remarked to his secretary, Ambrose Serle, that 'almost all the People of Parts & Spirit were in the Rebellion'. Serle himself, though a close friend of Galloway's and more sympathetic to the Tories than most British officials, remarked when told of Pennsylvania's loyal sentiments, 'But, alas, they all prate & profess much; but when You call upon them, they will *do* nothing.' Even Galloway, when questioned by Edmund Burke, admitted that nowhere did the people rise to join Howe when he 'liberated' a region, and that not many Loyalists had enlisted in the regular British forces. He explained this, however, on grounds that the Loyalists had been disarmed, and had never been supported by the British when they had attempted to resist the Congress.[12]

Still, there seems little doubt that Lord Howe and his brother did over-estimate American support for the Revolution, while at the same time underestimating the obduracy of the Revolution itself. By neglecting the Tories because they seemed weak, the British made them weaker still. There was also, of course, in the British attitude towards the Loyalists, a good deal of the professional soldier's distrust of civilians, along with a certain contempt for Americans generally. Some of the difficulties that arose between the Loyalists and the British were reminiscent of the troubles between the provincials and the British in the earlier colonial wars. The Tories in British service persistently complained of the menial duties

---

[12] E. H. Tatum, Jr., ed., *The American Journal of Ambrose Serle, Secretary to Lord Howe, 1776–1778* (San Marino, 1940), pp. 6, 164; Galloway, *Examination . . . before the House of Commons*, pp. 71–72; id., *Reply to Howe*, pp. 36–37.

given them, and were, in turn, mocked by the revolutionists on the same grounds:

> Come, gentlemen Tories, firm, loyal and true,
> Here are axes and shovels and something to do!
> For the sake of our king,
> Come labor and sing.[13]

The Tories occasionally conceded their own military failings, however. Edward Winslow, who eventually became Muster-Master-General of the Loyalist forces, admitted that many Loyalists were reluctant to serve outside their own provinces, and that others enlisted for a fixed term and at its expiration wanted to 'change their ground'. Still others, he wrote, were unaccustomed to military discipline, 'unaccustomed to severity, have been made miserable and unhappy'. At the same time Winslow wrote that the Loyalist troops, 'if duly encouraged would have been much more respectable in point of numbers than they are at present, and if properly employed would have contributed largely towards suppressing the rebellion'. He complained of lack of British co-operation in recruiting volunteers, and in providing supplies.

In some of his strictures against the British Winslow found himself, apparently without embarrassment, on the side of his enemies, the revolutionists. 'Bold as the assertion may appear', he wrote, 'I venture to affirm that the British have gained near as much from their observations of the Provincial and American Troops as the latter have acquired from them.' He observed that the British had learned 'to Tree' from the Americans, and he even went so far as to gloat a little over Burgoyne's defeat by raw American recruits whom he had scorned.[14]

The Loyalists appear to have been less surprised by Burgoyne's surrender than were the British. They recognized it, however, as a powerful blow to their cause. 'This', James Allen

---

[13] Quoted, Van Tyne, *Loyalists*, p. 147.
[14] *Winslow Papers*, pp. 40–44, 67–70.

wrote of the news of Saratoga, 'will raise the drooping spirits of our people, till now quite sunk.'[15] Even more than by Saratoga, however, the Loyalists were dismayed by Howe's inactivity during the following winter, while Washington lay nearly helpless at Valley Forge; and they were shocked by what seemed the pointless evacuation of Philadelphia late the following spring. Tory complaints against Howe grew more and more bitter, few of them having the good humour of this little Loyalist verse, popular during the spring of 1778:

> Awake, arouse, Sir Billy,
> There's forage in the plain,
> Ah, leave your little Filly,
> And open the campaign.[16]

Late in 1777 Hutchinson wrote cautiously: 'The clamour increases against the Howes, who ought to be heard before they are condemned.' Most of Hutchinson's fellow Tories saw no reason to wait to condemn Sir William Howe. Judge Jones wrote that Howe's proper reward for his services would have been an execution, and Isaac Wilkins wrote to Chandler that he hoped to hear that Howe was hanged. The Tories were overjoyed when Howe was finally removed from his command and replaced by Sir Henry Clinton whom, at first, they trusted. James Allen noted that Clinton sought out and consulted the Loyalists, who had had little intercourse with Howe. Galloway contrasted Howe's advice that the Loyalists submit to the Congress, with Clinton's assurance 'that the game was not up', and that the Loyalists certainly should not go over to the enemy.[17]

---

[15] 'Diary of James Allen', p. 295.
[16] Quoted, Jones, *History*, i. 716.
[17] Hutchinson, *Diary*, ii. 172, 228; 'Diary of James Allen', p. 438; Galloway, *Examination . . . before the House of Commons*, pp. 36–38. Loyalist criticisms of General Howe, other than those mentioned above, may be found in Boucher, 'Letters', ix. 240; Van Schaack, *Life*, pp. 169–84; Jones, *History*, i. 189–95, 237; and *Winslow Papers*, pp. 36–37.

As the war dragged on, however, and Clinton proved less competent and no more aggressive than Howe had been, the Loyalists despaired of him too. Convinced that there was no remedy for the Revolution but to wage war against it, the Loyalists grew less and less patient with British inactivity. In the summer of 1778 Edward Winslow wrote to a friend:

It is said that Gen. Clinton is certain to come with the army by land to New York, if so they must kick up a hell of a dust in the Jersies. I really imagined soon after your departure that something very capital would have taken place ere this, but there has been such a damnable series of treating and retreating—Pidling, conciliating & commissioning, that fighting (which is the only remedy for the American disorder) has been totally suspended . . .[18]

When Clinton did bring his army to New York, by sea and without fighting, the Loyalists were astonished at his determined refusal to venture outside the defences around the city. Jones observed that in 1780 Clinton had 20,000 men idle in New York, while Washington lay fifty miles way with 7,000 men. Washington's men were even allowed, Jones wrote, to collect forage unmolested almost within sight of the British lines in Westchester County.[19] Commenting in 1780 on Clinton's refusal to support a Tory plan to raise a brigade of New England Loyalists, Winslow wrote:

The stupor which seemed to seize his Excellency [Clinton] & which nothing short of a super-natural event can rouse him from, effectually prevented any [Loyalist] military enterprises. The defensive system which he adopted was so complete that there was no possibility of advancing without the lines and it must have been a very active and determined deserter that could get within them. 'Tis unnecessary to observe that a campaign in which all the Grenadiers of the Army are employed in digging, and half the Dragoons foraging on foot among peaceable inhabitants, could not be productive of capital acquisitions . . . For my own part as I never despond, I indulge a hope that I shall yet have a chance of

[18] *Winslow Papers*, pp. 30–31.
[19] Jones, *History*, i. 362, 366–7.

seeing a General that's neither a Rebel or a Histerical Fool at the Head of a British Army in America.[20]

As further evidence of Clinton's irresoluteness, Jones cited his failure to exploit the mutiny of the Pennsylvania and New Jersey militia early in 1781. Had the British, Jones wrote, marched from Staten Island to Princeton, they might well have been able to rout Washington's demoralized army. Instead Clinton stayed quiet, and presented such undignified terms to the mutineers that they resumed their allegiance to the Congress.[21]

Clinton, it may be said, did not fully trust the Loyalists, and was constantly warned against them by his officers. Early in 1781, for example, General Charles Grey wrote to him, 'For God's sake put no confidence in any of those *loyal* Americans near you. Many are spies upon you, sending home what they know will please.' Faced with the problem of how to use the Loyalist regiments in British service without incorporating them in his regular forces, Clinton unwisely allowed them, in the later years of the war, to organize raids into territory held by the Congress. These freebooting expeditions along the coast, combined with the partisan warfare of the frontier Tories, did much to embitter the revolutionists against the Loyalists. Some of the Tories themselves were indignant at the depredations of the Loyalist raiding parties. Jones wrote that the raids along the New England coast and up the Delaware 'were of no service to the general cause. They answered the purpose of plunderers, robbers, and marauders.' Jones thought that the atrocities of the Tories were, in general, worse than those of the rebels, observing that the rebel raiders seldom burned private houses as the Tories often did. Tories were themselves sometimes victims of Loyalist raiders: Ralph Wormeley and Philip Grymes in Virginia, for example, were mercilessly plundered by Tory privateers from New York.[22]

[20] *Winslow Papers*, pp. 64–65.   [21] Jones, *History*, ii. 179–83.
[22] Eckenrode, *The Revolution in Virginia*, p. 255; Jones, *History*, i. 236,

Charges of piracy and plundering became more frequent on all sides as the war grew more bitter. Jones compared British behaviour in this respect unfavourably with American, noting that the British destroyed several libraries in New York which the Americans had scrupulously protected. At Newport British soldiers were accused of plundering Loyalists, and a Committee of the Continental Congress affirmed that the British plundered Whig and Tory indiscriminately in New Jersey, a view shared by the Loyalists. On Staten Island the British were even accused of singling out the Tories for abuse, and of cursing them for having caused the war.[23]

One persistent Loyalist grievance against the British was that they would not restore civil government in the areas they controlled. This was particularly galling in New York under a British occupation that lasted seven years. The New York Tories also resented, as much as the Whigs, the billeting of British soldiers in private houses. Jones, describing the inconveniences of life in New York under the British military government, mentioned the case of a respectable New Yorker who was given 300 lashes by a court martial for having struck a British subaltern during an argument. He also, rather less convincingly, pleaded the case of a 'young gentleman of fortune' who was imprisoned by the British for having kicked a Negro driver employed by the Army.[24]

The Loyalists behind the British lines, despite all their vexations, seem to have fared better than their brethren who remained in areas under the control of the Congress. Of these, there were perhaps hundreds of thousands whose loyalty to the Crown was passive by reason of habit or conviction, sex or age. Many wished not to take sides, like James Allen of Philadelphia, who wrote, 'Many people who disapprove Indepen-

302, 315; Boyd, *Joseph Galloway*, p. 77; St. John Crèvecœur, *Letters from an American Farmer*, ed. W. P. Trent (New York, 1904), p. 312.

[23] Jones, *History*, i. 114, 121–2, 136; Galloway, *Letters to a Nobleman*, pp. 43–45; 5 *Am. Arch.* i. 1110–12; Van Tyne, *Loyalists*, pp. 247–9.

[24] Ibid., pp. 248–50; Jones, *History*, i. 354; ii. 83–85; Van Schaack, *Life*, p. 253.

dence have no other wish than to remain at peace, & secure in their persons without influencing the minds of others.' Early in the war neutrality was tolerated in many areas, especially in the Middle Colonies. Allen, for example, was able, during the autumn of 1776, to set out from Philadelphia with the Reverend William Smith as a companion, 'thro' mere curiosity to view the state of both armies'. On their tour Smith and Allen visited both the British and General Washington; through the heavy fighting of that autumn, Allen wrote, he remained 'a calm spectator of the civil War'.[25]

All through the war there were a few privileged Tories who stayed quietly at home, unmolested by the Revolution. Some of the most distinguished gentlemen of Virginia were Loyalists, notably William Byrd of Westover and Lord Fairfax, who were protected in their opinions by the vast respect Virginia accorded its gentry. There was no other Loyalist quite like Thomas, sixth Lord Fairfax. He had been born in the preceding century, was related to German royalty, and had served as a Colonel of the Blues, before settling finally in America in 1747. He owned, in addition to extensive properties in England, nearly one-quarter of the settled area of Virginia, some 9,000 square miles lying between the Potomac and Rappahannock Rivers. He lived at 'Greenway Court', unmolested though not untroubled by the war, and died in his eighty-ninth year after hearing of Cornwallis's surrender. 'Come, Joe!' he is alleged to have said to his servant, 'carry me to my bed, for it is high time for me to die'.[26]

While there were a few Tories, like Lord Fairfax, too important to molest, there were many too insignificant to be troubled for their opinions. Some of the most quiet and unobtrusive Loyalists were also the most implacable, like the Quaker historian of Pennsylvania, Robert Proud, who, in 1806, was still able to write of 'this country, since called, The United

[25] 'Diary of James Allen', pp. 191–3.
[26] Curwen, *Journal*, pp. 601–11; *Dictionary of American Biography*, ed. A. Johnson and D. Malone (20 vols., New York, 1931 et seq.), vi. 255–7.

States'. Proud wrote that his sedentary life, 'to which I have been thought to be naturally too much addicted, . . . has been a great Means of singularly preserving me from imminent Danger'. Despite the 'Anarchy and Tyranny' of the times, Proud wrote that he had been left alone, since he lived 'in a very private and retired Way, even like a Person dead amidst the Confusions'.[27]

Most Loyalists who remained in areas under the control of the Congress did not fare so well as Lord Fairfax or Proud. Even when passive, they were generally deprived of all civil rights. They could not collect debts or act as guardians or executors. They were forbidden to buy or sell land, and in some cases, even to will their property. In most of the new states the Loyalists were not allowed to practise law; in Pennsylvania they could not serve as druggists or apothecaries. In Connecticut a law of 1776 provided that any person who wrote or spoke against the Congress or against acts of the Connecticut Assembly could be fined, imprisoned, or disfranchised. Most other states passed similar laws. Tories who were regarded as especially dangerous or malignant were imprisoned, sometimes under appalling conditions, as in the case of those who were held in the Simsbury mine in Connecticut. Other Tories were sent, sometimes as hostages, into distant states.[28]

In the latter years of the war much of the correspondence between Tories came to be a comparison of respective losses and suffering. When Samuel Curwen, who had gone to England, wrote to his old friend William Pynchon, complaining of the hardships of the Loyalists in exile, Pynchon wrote back, 'If you knew half the inconveniences your continuance here would have occasioned, it would surely lessen your discontent.' Pynchon went on to complain of the loss of his business and of the forced sale of his house and lands. Thus reduced, he wrote, he still could not 'freely nor safely walk the streets,

[27] 'Autobiography of Robert Proud', *Pennsylvania Magazine of History and Biography*, xiii. 434; 'Letters', xxxiv. 63–64.
[28] Van Tyne, *Loyalists*, pp. 193–200, 235–6.

by reason of . . . the uncontrolled rancor of some men'. On the other hand, there were Loyalists who managed to keep a sense of humour amidst their difficulties. The Reverend Mather Byles of Boston, although nearly seventy years old at the beginning of the war, was threatened with banishment and put under guard. The guard was later taken away, then restored, and finally removed again, which led Byles to write that 'he was guarded, reguarded, and disreguarded'.[29]

The passive Loyalists who desired to remain aloof from the war found neutrality increasingly difficult. James Allen, after his calm inspection of the warring armies, offended some 'violent Whigs' by entertaining captured British officers. Although he denied being a Tory ('under which name is included every one disinclined to Independence tho' ever so warm a friend to constitutional liberty and the old cause'), Allen was arrested by the Philadelphia Committee and threatened with exile to North Carolina as a disaffected person. Despite his release, he was thoroughly frightened for his safety. He complained that 'The most discreet, passive, & respectable characters are dragged forth', and that there was much talk of taking Tory hostages. He managed for a while to enjoy the company of some of his old Whig friends, writing that 'we endeavour to banish politics'. Finally, however, even though he signed an oath of allegiance to the Continental Congress, Allen was charged with treason.[30]

Of all the changes produced by the Revolution, none impressed the Tories so much as the rise of the lowly and the fall of the great. That, as Allen wrote, 'the most insignificant now lord it with impunity & without discretion over the most respectable characters' seemed proof that the times were out of joint. Usually the Tories observed these social changes in personal terms. 'Everything I see', wrote Jonathan Sewell, 'is laughable, cursable, and damnable; my pew in the church is converted into a pork tub; my house into a den of rebels,

[29] Curwen, *Journal*, pp. 227–8, 494–5.
[30] 'Diary of James Allen', pp. 193, 288, 427, 438–41.

thieves & lice; my farm in possession of the very worst of all God's creation; my few debts all gone to the devil with my debtors. . . . All this is *right*, says Doctor Pangloss, & this is the best of all possible worlds.'[31]

The new riches and aspirations of their once meek neighbours aroused the scorn of the Tory gentry, especially when these new acquisitions were their own former possessions. It seemed most unjust that 'dear Mr. Hallowell's clothes pass the house every Sunday on the back of a nasty great cooper', or that persons 'who had not money enough for shoes for their feet, are now riding in coaches of their own in Boston.' The loss of their coaches, indeed, seems to have been particularly galling to Tories who had had them, coaches having been the most conspicuous symbols of social rank in the old colonies. When Hutchinson wrote that 'Washington, it is said, rides in my coach at Cambridge', he was not merely recording a material loss, in this case, to a social equal; he was implying a change of sovereignty. Grace Galloway, Joseph Galloway's wife, seems to have stood the loss of her house, family, and friends better than the sight of her own carriage driven for another: 'as I was walking in the Rain', she wrote piteously, 'My own Chariot Drove by. I own that I then thought it hard but I Kept Up pretty well but when I turn'd into the alley My dear child came into My Mind & what she wou'd say to see her Mamma walking 5 squares in the rain at Night like a common Woman . . . I dare not think.' Later, in a more assertive mood, Mrs. Galloway wrote fiercely that 'all will be right yet & I shall ride when these Harpies walk as they Use to do'.[32]

However much social change there was, it was not enough, in the more settled parts of the colonies, to persuade even the Tories that society itself was in danger of destruction. In the

[31] 'Diary of James Allen', p. 196; 'Letters of Jonathan Sewell', *Proceedings*, Massachusetts Historical Society, 2nd series, x. 414.

[32] 'Diary of Grace Crowdon Galloway', *Pennsylvania Magazine of History and Biography*, lv. 57, 61; *Winslow Papers*, p. 25; Curwen, *Journal*, p. 215; Hutchinson, *Diary*, i. 557.

frontier regions this was not true. There the war took on increasingly a savage character, especially in the Southern states. Whatever political issues had divided Whigs and Tories in earlier times were gradually lost in the confusion of Indian raids, massacres, family feuds, and plain banditry. Whigs and Tories changed sides as convenience dictated, and as the forces of the Revolution gradually consolidated themselves and began to recover the frontier country, 'Tory' tended more and more to become a title taken by outlaws.

The familial and vengeful nature of strife in the back country may be illustrated by two minor incidents of the war between Whig and Tory: in North Carolina a Whig named John Cornelison was attacked by a band of Tories, beaten, shot, and pushed into his own fireplace, from which he was pulled out dead by his wife. A relative of Cornelison's named Spiney learned the name of one of the Tories and followed the man into Tennessee. Finding the man living alone in a log cabin, Spiney pushed the muzzle of his gun through a crack between the logs and shot him down, returning then to North Carolina.[33]

In South Carolina one of the Tory partisan leaders was Major William Cunningham, known as 'Bloody Bill'. Cunningham's father was beaten and kicked, and his epileptic brother whipped to death by a Whig captain, one William Ritchie. Cunningham thereupon walked all the way from Savannah to District Ninety-Six, and killed Ritchie, beginning a series of retaliatory murders. After one engagement in which Cunningham's band had captured a number of Whigs, 'Each of Cunningham's men singled out whomsoever among the prisoners had been guilty of murdering any of his relatives, and killed him forthwith.'[34]

To Hector St. John Crèvecœur, the gentle, Quakerish Frenchman who had settled on a farm in Orange County, New York, the violence of civil war in the back country seemed the natural result of the principles of the Revolution.

[33] DeMond, *Loyalism in North Carolina*, p. 122. [34] Curwen, *Journal*, p. 645.

Unlike most English Americans, Crèvecœur combined a keen appreciation of the simplicity of American life with an alarm for the weakness of American society. Living near the frontier, he watched with horror as the frail bonds of western society broke apart. 'The rage of civil discord', he wrote, 'hath advanced among us with an astounding rapidity. Every opinion is changed; . . . every mode of organization which linked us before as men and as citizens, is now altered.'

It was the Revolution itself, Crèvecœur thought, which had destroyed the respect for law without which no community could endure. 'When,' he wrote, 'from whatever motives, the laws are no longer respected; when . . . all the social bonds are loosened, the same effects will follow. This is now the case with us: the son is armed against the father, the brother against the brother, family against family.' To Crèvecœur the Revolution was a gross deception, its grievances fantasies; it was a disease which he tried to bear 'as you would a fever or a cold'. Describing the ravages of war, he wrote, 'But what can you expect when law, government, morality are become silent? . . . When men are artfully brought into a chaos.' 'I wish', he decided finally, 'for a change of place . . . what is man when no longer connected with society; or when he finds himself surrounded by a convulsed and a half dissolved one?'[35]

After the spring of 1776 Loyalist opinion towards the new American government changed little, except to increase in vehemence. The main charge the Loyalists made against the Congress was that of tyranny. In his *Letters of Papinian*, published in Rivington's *Royal Gazette*, Charles Inglis attacked the Revolution with a violence typical of Tory inculpations in the latter years of the war. Every man, he wrote, had a tyrant at his door, was subject to a veritable Inquisition, carried out by Committee and Congress. The leading principle of the Revolution, as Inglis saw it, was mob intimidation, evidenced by the mistreatment of the Loyalists, who, he wrote, were stripped of their property, their freedom, and even their lives,

[35] Crèvecœur, *Letters*, pp. 281–2; id., *Sketches*, pp. 178–9, 229, 279.

all without regular legal process. His most bitter indignation, Inglis reserved, however, for the French alliance: 'You have sold the birth-right of British subjects to become MORTGAGED to France', he wrote, '... You plow and sow, you labour and toil, you fight and bleed for France, and for those who have betrayed you to France—Your Congress.'[36]

The Tories generally made much of the French alliance, usually flavouring their strictures with vigorous anti-Catholic sentiments. It was claimed, for example, that crucifixes, rosaries, and casks of holy water were being imported by the French, along with such secular objects as dancing masters and dried frogs. It was hinted that Rhode Island, where the French were based, or some other part of America, had been ceded secretly to France.[37] The French alliance was, in fact, responsible for the appearance of a few, very late 'Loyalists', the most notable of whom was Silas Deane, who along with Benjamin Franklin and Arthur Lee had been one of the American commissioners to France.

Although he had been a faithful Whig, and a member of the First and Second Congresses, Deane seems to have had lurking Anglophile sentiments that were brought to life by his unpleasant experiences in France, and by what he regarded as the unfairness of the Congress in its dealings with him. He decided that America had to choose, not between independence and submission to Britain, but between dependence on Britain and dependence on France, and of these evils he infinitely preferred the former. 'The world', he wrote, 'is not so dependent on us—we are more dependent on our neighbors than they on us.' In France he had observed that the Americans were regarded as English, acted like Englishmen, and, despite the war, were always anxious to go to England. He concluded that America's relations with Britain rested on a fundamental cultural sameness that required some political expression. In

---

[36] Charles Inglis, *The Letters of Papinian* (London, 1779); Lydekker, *Life of Inglis*, p. 165.

[37] Van Tyne, *Loyalists*, pp. 154–5.

addition, he decided, partly perhaps from his own troubles with the Congress, that America was incapable of efficient self-government. Although angrily criticized in America for his views, Deane clung to them until after the war. 'Still', he wrote in 1781, 'things in America would be happier and we would enjoy greater liberties, subject to England.'[38]

[38] G. L. Clark, *Silas Deane* (New York, 1913), pp. 183–97.

CHAPTER VIII

The Refugees

OF all the Loyalists, those who spent the war years as refugees in England suffered, perhaps, the most exquisite spiritual anguish. Probably the largest single group of these people were New Englanders who had left when Boston was evacuated by the British. They were joined in England by a number of later migrants from the Middle Colonies, and a few from the South. Many of these men had belonged to the Tory establishment before the War: they had been judges and provincial councillors, Anglican clergymen, collectors of customs, and even royal governors. They had formed the Tory vanguard and, from having in earlier times, faithfully served and also resolutely used Britain for their own profit and advancement, they were now reduced to an abject dependence on British charity.

The refugees in England had various reasons for being there. A few, like Governor Hutchinson, hoped to influence British policy and share in the new arrangements they expected to be made for the colonies. Others had simply decided, like Samuel Curwen, to 'withdraw for a while from the storm'. 'I left my late peaceful home (in my sixtieth year)', Curwen wrote, 'in search of personal security and those rights which by the laws of God I ought to have enjoyed undisturbed there.'[1] Curwen's friend, Jonathan Sewell, had been alarmed and repelled by the revolutionary zeal of his countrymen, 'the whole troop', he wrote, 'rushing into the arms of Slavery, & all in honour of the afores[d] goddess Liberty, as Indians cut & mangle themselves to please the Devil'. He had been persuaded to leave Boston, Sewell wrote, by 'Musketry, bombs,

---

[1] Curwen, *Journal*, p. 25.

great guns, redoubts, lines, batterys, enfilades, battles, seiges, murder, plague, pestilence, famine, rebellion, & the Devil.'[2] In England the refugees hoped to find, not only safety, but an atmosphere of tolerance, and the personal respect they felt they deserved.

When Curwen arrived in England in the summer of 1775 he found 'an army of New Englanders' already there. He was taken to the New England Coffee House on Threadneedle Street, where the Tories met to pass the time, argue over the news, encourage one another's hopes, and exchange one another's troubles. He joined the New England Club which met for a weekly dinner at the Adelphi Tavern in the Strand. He sought out old acquaintances, was cordially received by Governor Hutchinson, had tea with John Copley, and met Benjamin West, whom he described as 'a most masterly hand in historic painting'. And then, after a week or two of meeting old friends and seeing the sights of London, Curwen, like almost all his fellows, began to feel a certain unease.[3]

The Loyalists were not disappointed in the magnificence of London, although most of them were, like other Americans of the day, shocked at its luxury and ostentation. They were also overwhelmed by its size: Van Schaack wrote that he felt like 'an atom' in London, and Jonathan Boucher's wife, Nelly, urged him to 'wait with her till the crowd should be gone past', until he explained that there was no more crowd than usual. Expecting everything to be grander and better than in America, the Loyalists found certain disappointments, to be sure. Van Schaack, although he thought London 'an epitome of the world', and much admired Westminster Abbey, disliked the vehemence of manner customary in the House of Commons, and was repelled by English pleasure-seeking. Curwen found English courts noisy, and was not impressed with Garrick; at the same time he observed that church services were more correct than in New England, and he described a per-

[2] 'Letters of Jonathan Sewell', p. 413.
[3] Curwen, *Journal*, pp. 30–31, 45, 51.

formance of Handel's *Messiah* at Covent Garden as 'exalted',
'noble', 'grand', and 'awfully majestic'.[4]

Jonathan Sewell seems to have taken English luxury quite
in his stride. 'I wish you were here Ned,' he wrote to a friend in
America, 'with Money enough in your pocket—you can have
no idea what a noble Country this is for a Gentleman—every
Thing is upon an immense Scale—whatever I have seen in my
own Country, is all Miniature, yankee-puppet-show . . . the
Wealth of this Country is truly astonishing, but unless a
Gentleman can get his Share of it, he has no Business here.'
Sewell's qualification of his encomium apparently had a basis
in his own experience, for on one occasion he was forced to
borrow ten guineas from Governor Hutchinson.[5]

Their spare American habits, as well as lack of money,
dimmed the lustre of the metropolis for many of the Loyalists.
Curwen, noting that some of his fellows 'affect to prefer this
country to their own', wrote, '*pour moi*, I wish for nothing
more than peace and to return thither'. England, he added,
'is, or might be, a paradise of delights for those who enjoy
a full purse, and are by education and habit formed to relish
its delights, amusements and pursuits; but for me America is
good enough.'[6]

Comparisons between England and America formed a topic
of inveterate discussion among the refugees. 'We had a dispute
after dinner,' Peggy Hutchinson wrote, 'which was the best
country—New England, or Old.' Peggy and her father preferred New England, Governor Hutchinson expressing his
preference in 'very strong terms'. Another Loyalist who preferred England was finally argued into silence. 'The men do
not please me here'; Peggy wrote, 'and Miss Murray and I
both agreed on our first arrival, that New England was the
only place for pretty fellows.' Besides, Peggy was distressed by

[4] Curwen, *Journal*, pp. 32–33, 39–40, 49; Van Schaack, *Life*, pp. 135, 161–2;
Boucher, *Reminiscences*, p. 143.

[5] *Winslow Papers*, pp. 13–14; Hutchinson, *Diary*, i. 542.

[6] Curwen, *Journal*, pp. 230–1.

the English climate, while her father noted reprovingly that in England 'it was a reproach to a man to be a serious christian'.[7]

Some of the Loyalists found it difficult to preserve one cherished illusion from damage: they were not universally awed by a close view of the King in whose name they had quarrelled with their countrymen. Curwen wrote dourly of George III: 'He is tall, square over the shoulders, large ugly mouth, talks a great deal, and shows his teeth too much; his countenance heavy and lifeless, with white eyebrows.' Even Hutchinson, while pleased with the King's attentions, found it difficult to communicate with him. He bristled when the King said to him, 'I see they threatened to pitch and feather you.' 'Tarr & feather, may it please your Majesty,' Hutchinson replied, 'but I don't remember that ever I was threatened with it.'[8]

English tolerance, on the other hand, the Loyalists discovered to have substance. Political arguments, Curwen wrote, were warm but 'without abuse or ill nature', and it was 'unfashionable' to quarrel over public matters. 'The doctrine of toleration', he concluded, 'if not better understood, is, thank God, better practised here than in America.' Sewell, emphatic as always, wrote to a friend in New England that while politics 'is in your Land of *Liberty* a subject too sacred to be meddled with by the profane vulgar, . . . in the Land of *Slaves* a cobbler or a chimney sweeper claims & exercises freely, as his undoubted right, the privilege of arraining, examining, judging & condemning the conduct of the King's Ministers, of the Parliament, & even of the King himself.'[9]

To their surprise, and sometimes dismay, however, the Loyalists found that English tolerance extended to the Revolution itself. 'There appears', wrote Curwen, 'to be a tenderness in the minds of many here for America.' This sympathy for their enemies the Tories often found among those 'middle

[7] Hutchinson, *Diary*, i. 200–1, 232, 276, 278.
[8] Ibid. i. 164; Curwen, *Journal*, p. 319.
[9] Ibid., p. 38; 'Letters of Jonathan Sewell', p. 425.

ranks' of Englishmen whom in other respects they found to be the most congenial of their hosts. Curwen described a Quaker he met as 'a sensible man and a *warm American*, as most of the middling classes are'. Another time he met a friendly gunmaker in Bristol, who was to make rifles for the government, 'but is in principle an antiministerialist, as is the whole town'. Van Schaack observed that 'vast numbers' in England avowed the cause of America, and even after the war wrote that 'the people at large love the Americans, though the tender ties are dissolved'.[10]

The Loyalists were naturally much concerned with whether or not the English were disposed to make them welcome. Van Schaack, who was a personable young man, found the English 'hospitable, sociable, and well-bred, particularly the women'. Curwen, however, who described himself as 'old, small and infirm', wrote that the English were 'too proud or reserved' to make friends with easily. Few of these Americans, even among the English-born, seem to have found themselves perfectly at home in England. Jonathan Boucher wrote of the Bishop of London and the Archbishop of Canterbury, 'They are cold & formal, & seem to think they do Wonders, when they give you a Dinner.' Boucher concluded that he was 'fit only for America'. There, he wrote, 'I have some Character & Note—here, every Body I see eclipses Me . . . here I am all to begin again.' Boucher, being an Englishman and comparatively young, could and did 'begin again'. This was hardly possible for most of the refugees, however. They found England, with all its tempting riches, a society closed to them. The charms of oligarchy were perceptibly diminished when viewed from outside the golden circle.[11]

As time passed most of the refugees became increasingly critical of things English, sensitive to real or fancied slights, and morbidly conscious of what Curwen called their 'uneasy

---

[10] Curwen, *Journal*, pp. 35, 38, 74–75; Van Schaack, *Life*, p. 326.
[11] Ibid., p. 150; Curwen, *Journal*, pp. 63, 290; Boucher, 'Letters', viii. 344–5.

abode in this country of aliens'. Having much time and, most of them, little money, they wandered away from London, looking for congenial and inexpensive places to live, looking, in fact, for Marblehead or Salem, Charleston, Philadelphia, or New York. One wrote of their quest, 'Some men are always happy where they are, some where they have been, and some where they shall be; and yet we are none of us satisfied with either past, present, or to come.' None except the Scots seem to have liked Scotland, few went to Ireland, and few liked the North, Curwen writing of Manchester that 'the people are remarkable for coarseness of feature, and the language is unintelligible'. Surprisingly, not many seem to have examined the eastern counties, although Van Schaack was struck with the American manners and 'strong traces of the New England accent' in Bedfordshire. Perhaps the Tories' favourite place was Bristol, where, as Hutchinson noted approvingly, 'you might pick out a set of Boston Selectmen from any of their churches'. In Bristol they could count on the hospitality and interest of Josiah Tucker, and Curwen was pleased beyond measure when the Bishop of Bristol, in a 'seasonable and candid discourse', called the war with America '"a civil war," and the Americans "our unhappy fellow-subjects"'. 'I shall set out next Monday, bag & baggage for Bristol', Sewell wrote, 'there to remain till the restoration of peace, & perhaps till the restoration of all things.'[12]

It was, of course, their loss of occupation and social standing, their loss of *place* in society, that made the refugees miserable in spirit. 'Inability to provide for one's own support', Curwen wrote, 'is a mortifying consideration . . . Without something in pursuit, rightly or wrongly estimated worthy, life is insipid;—a connection with my fellow men, constant employment, and a much less sum would render me more pleased with the world and myself, than the supplies I receive whilst I dream the blank of life along, unknowing and un-

[12] Curwen, *Journal*, pp. 58, 89, 136, 269; Van Schaack, *Life*, p. 154; Hutchinson, *Diary*, ii. 148; 'Letters of Jonathan Sewell', p. 420.

known . . . Man was formed for useful action.'[13] Another Loyalist addressed himself bitterly to the same question: 'Well informed Americans do not place all happiness in opulence, or splendid shew. Had their souls been bare enough to be directed by such groveling principles, you would not have been troubled with their persons . . . A personal notice is what gentlemen exceedingly value . . .'.[14]

Governor Hutchinson's experiences illuminate nicely the plight of the Loyalists in England. As one of the earliest and most important refugees, he received, at first, considerable attention. After his long interview with the King, immediately upon his arrival, he was invited to accept a baronetcy (which he declined for 'want of fortune'), and an honorary degree at Oxford. He had interviews with Lords North and Rockingham, and received calls from most of the other ministers and would-be ministers, including Hillsborough, Mansfield, Hardwicke, Dartmouth, and Wedderburn. 'My reception here', he wrote, 'exceeded everything I could imagine.'[15]

Pleased with the notice of the great, Hutchinson considered joining the English establishment that seemed so open to him. 'I am sometimes tempted', he wrote, 'to endeavour to forget that I am an American, and to turn my views to a provision for what remains of life in England.' Everyone, he wrote, advised him to settle in England, but, he confessed almost sadly, 'the passion for my native country returns'. As the months passed, however, Hutchinson received less consideration. Although still consulted faithfully by his fellow refugees, he was increasingly disregarded by the government. After a year and a half in England he was able to write without illusion, 'We Americans are plenty here, and very cheap. Some of us at first coming, are apt to think ourselves of importance, but other people do not think so, and few, if any of us are much consulted, or enquired after.' He asked his friends not

[13] Curwen, *Journal*, pp. 212–13.
[14] Quoted, Boyd, *Joseph Galloway*, pp. 75–76; ascribed to Galloway.
[15] Hutchinson, *Diary*, i. 157–87.

to address their letters to him as formerly: 'Pray leave off *His Excell^y* in y^r directions, for everybody laughs at such things here.'[16]

Deprived of his importance and denied a place in society, Hutchinson became militantly American, or rather New Englandish, his affection for New England ways increasing with his discontent. 'I had rather live at Milton than at Kew', he wrote; and again, 'we live as much in the N. Eng^d way as ever we can'. 'I meet with no diversions or entertainments', he wrote to his son, 'that are so agreeable to me as what I could find at home.' Meeting a New-England-born gentleman who took little interest in his own American background, Hutchinson was first astonished and then alarmed. 'My thoughts day and night are upon New England', he wrote, and then declared vigorously, 'New England is wrote upon my heart in as strong characters as Calais was upon Queen Mary's.' 'I shall yet live and die among them', he wrote of his old neighbours, 'and I trust, recover their esteem.'[17]

Having little else to do, Hutchinson often found himself in a mood of reverie, which came easily to him, he wrote, 'from my situation at this time of life, so unexpected to me, three thousand miles from my country and friends, so that every scene has the appearance of a dream, rather than a reality'. Another time he wrote, 'In this kind of life the days and nights pass incredibly swift, and I am six months older and nearer to my own death, . . . and it appears like the dream of a night.' Like many of his fellow exiles Hutchinson began to wonder where he might die, rather than live; even here his preference was unshakeable: 'I had rather die in a little country farm house in N. England', he wrote, 'than in the best Nobleman's seat in Old England.' He was denied this, along with his other hopes, and died in London in 1780, his funeral procession passing through streets filled with mobs and smoke from the Gordon riots.[18]

<hr/>

[16] Hutchinson, *Diary*, i. 215, 231; ii. 40.   [17] Ibid. i. 261, 281, 283–4, 352.
[18] Ibid. 351, 356; ii. 156; Hosmer, *Life of Hutchinson*, p. 349.

Homesickness became an endemic disease among the English exiles. The longings of the New Englanders, in particular, seem to have focused on the nearly unobtainable delicacies of their native province. Curwen ceremoniously presented a 'Mass. Bay apple' to a fellow refugee, and Hutchinson once wrote an appeal to his son for several bushels of cranberries, including minute instructions on how they should be picked and shipped. Jonathan Sewell added hickory nuts to the list of things utterly desirable: 'I have wrote Chip ... desiring him to send me by the return Bristol Ships, a few Newtown pippins, Shagbarks & Cranberrys—do spur him up. You can't conceive what a regale Newtown pippins, Shagbarks & Cranberrys would be to us Refugees.'[19]

The Loyalists in England seldom admitted a desire to return to America except as vindicated patriots. Occasionally, however, one would compromise his pride in order to solicit mercy for one weaker than himself. Sewell, for example, wrote to a Tory friend who had already returned to Massachusetts, hoping she would obtain permission for a mutual friend to go back too, 'for ... he can neither live nor die in peace but in Salem, his once happy seat'. Sewell was careful to add, however, 'tho' I do not know another American Loyalist now in England, except Aunt Jenny, who would return if they might'. Samuel Quincy wrote that 'a return to my native country I cannot be reconciled to until I am convinced that I am as well thought of as I know I deserve to be. I shall ever rejoice in its prosperity, but am too proud to live despised where I was once respected.' Curwen, on the other hand, did not qualify his wish to return, writing that 'nothing but the hopes of once more revisiting my native soil, enjoying my old friends within my own little domain has hitherto supported my drooping courage.'[20]

It would seem, at first sight, that the refugees in England were ungrateful towards the country which had not only

[19] Curwen, *Journal*, p. 228; Hutchinson, *Diary*, i. 200-1; *Winslow Papers*, p. 61.
[20] 'Letters of Jonathan Sewell', pp. 422-3; Curwen, *Journal*, pp. 161, 570.

welcomed them, but supported most of them generously. Emotionally, however, the Loyalists were correct in feeling excluded from English society, and perhaps they may be forgiven in part their occasional bitterness towards England. Their criticisms of the English grew sharper as it became increasingly clear that England would not suppress the Revolution. They had always been shocked by English luxury and profligacy; now they began to comment on what seemed to them the arrogance and decadence of England. Gratified at first by English calm, they gradually decided that this was only apathy and complacence. 'I am astonished', Hutchinson wrote irritably, 'at seeing so little concern upon the minds of so great a part of the people—I might almost say all, when it appears to me that the nation is in such imminent hazard of some grand convulsion.' Curwen came to the conclusion that England had 'sunk into too selfish, degenerate, luxurious a sloth' ever to recover and win the war. Noting the frivolity of the upper classes, and the sullen indifference of the lower, he confidently predicted the destruction of the parent country.[21]

Like the Loyalists serving with the British in America, the Tory exiles had ambivalent attitudes towards the war. Sometimes, in vindictive moments, they prayed for the destruction of America, usually, it is true, the destruction of provinces other than their own. Even Hutchinson criticized British 'laxity and kindness' in forbearing to use Indians against the Americans, and rejoiced at the Indian attacks in the South. 'Ten years ago', he wrote, 'I should have felt for the poor inhabitants of Virginia if I had heard that the Creeks and Cherokee Indians had fallen upon them, but I have lost those feelings now and rather was pleased to read the account.' Hutchinson, while fearing the 'destruction of poor Boston', hoped the Hessians would humble the 'modern Babylon' of Philadelphia, and he even advocated the employment of Russian mercenaries in America.[22]

[21] Curwen, *Journal*, pp. 169, 179; Hutchinson, *Diary*, ii. 291.
[22] L. Einstein, *Divided Loyalties: Americans in England During the War*

Nowhere are the mixed feelings of the exiles more evident than in their views of the comparative military prowess of Britain and America. Shortly after the battle of Bunker Hill, when Lord Hardwicke mentioned to him his surprise at American military skill, Hutchinson commented drily: 'I have had this opinion of Americans that, although we never rise to the top in any art or science, yet we attain to a mediocrity with as great rapidity as any people whatever.'[23] After hearing a British officer dismiss the Americans with contempt, Curwen wrote fiercely, 'It is my earnest wish the despised Americans may convince these conceited islanders, that without regular standing armies our continent can furnish brave soldiers and judicious and expert commanders . . . It piques my pride, I confess, to hear us called "*our colonies, our plantations,*" . . . as if our property and persons were absolutely theirs.' Curwen even managed to derive a certain satisfaction from the gloomy news of Cornwallis's surrender, 'perhaps the first of its kind', he wrote, 'that ever befell this haughty America-despising people'. Yet, when it came to fighting the French, Curwen was a Briton, writing hopefully of the 'superiority of our English sailors'.[24]

Aside from a few congenital optimists like Jonathan Sewell and Charles Inglis, the Loyalists, whether in Britain or America, seemed to have despaired of a conclusive British victory after France's entry into the war in 1778. Although they respected Cornwallis, were grateful for his civilities, and observed that he was 'ever vigilant and active in whatever was committed to his care', the Loyalists seem not to have been much impressed by his victories in the Southern states, nor much surprised by his surrender at Yorktown. Early in the war Hutchinson had written that 'a strange fatality attends this affair in every stage of it'. Later Judge Jones wrote, 'A

of Independence (London, 1933), pp. 178–9; Jones, *Loyalists of Massachusetts*, p. 173; Hutchinson, *Diary*, ii. 156.

[23] Quoted, Einstein, *Divided Loyalties*, p. 176.
[24] Curwen, *Journal*, pp. 90–91, 184, 326.

fatality attended all the British proceedings during the whole of the American war.' The sense of fatality, which may itself have been fatal, seems to have settled almost universally in the minds of the Tories, where events fed it and gave it substance.[25]

As early as August 1778 Hutchinson wrote in despair, 'Why don't Government withdraw its forces, and leave the Americans to that Independence which the Ministry seem to expect they will attain to?' Curwen decided that 'the sun of Britain is past the meridian and declining fast to the west', and began to wonder what life was like in the United States. 'For whatever you warm transatlantic loyalists may think', he wrote to a friend in New York, 'it is probable, however the general war may terminate, there never will be established such a degree of British governmental authority in North America as will cause much matter of triumph to American refugees.'[26]

Still much concerned, in his austere and introspective way, with the consistency of his own views, Peter Van Schaack began in 1779 to argue himself out of his Loyalism in the same systematic manner he had argued himself in. He was suspicious of the optimism of some of his Loyalist and British friends. 'There is nothing so absurd,' he wrote, 'which people having the same wishes, and the same interests, and associating together, and with no persons of contrary sentiments, may not persuade themselves to *think, believe,* or *to do.*' Having his own interests and wishes, and associating mainly with himself, Van Schaack decided that Britain could not win the war: 'A man sanguine of the success of British arms in the country will begin to *doubt* at New-York. In England he will despair.'

Unhurriedly Van Schaack speculated on the effects of the loss of the war. It might well be for the best, he decided. Perhaps the British 'must be d——d to be politically saved'. The loss of the colonies, he thought, might lead to the collapse of

[25] Jones, *History*, i. 355; ii. 185; Galloway, *Letters to a Nobleman*, pp. 78–79; Hutchinson, *Diary*, ii. 95; Van Tyne, *Loyalists*, p. 247. Jones did enter a final, formal protest at Clinton's inactivity when Washington and Rochambeau marched south. *History*, ii. 206–7.

[26] Hutchinson, *Diary*, ii. 212; Curwen, *Journal*, pp. 197, 323–4.

the 'artificial system of politics' that had corrupted England. Then men 'of the middling classes' might be able to enter and revivify public life. In any case the war was now 'merely *British*', and its continuance due merely to British vindictiveness. Therefore, Van Schaack wrote righteously, 'my connection with the parent country is dissolved. I am to consider the happiness of *that* country [America], not the aggrandizement of *this*.' Consistent to the last, Van Schaack concluded, 'if I can return, . . . I shall be so good a subject of the new government as I ever was of the old.'[27]

After the surrender at Yorktown, the Loyalists found themselves with little save their loyalty. They realized that this had become woefully depreciated in value, worth less in some ways than that Continental currency they had scorned. They differed among themselves, however, about what to do with it. Whether to abandon it, or hoard it, or spend it, or try to exchange it for more useful coin. In New York, almost the only place where it was legal tender, loyalty was freely spent. During the autumn of 1781, beginning with celebrations of the visit of Prince William Henry,[28] New York indulged in a veritable royalist orgy, even more desperate than foolish. All season loyal New Yorkers were 'up to ears and eyes in Concerts, Plays, Balls and Charades'. At a celebration of the King's birthday elaborate fireworks were set off, the most notable piece representing 'George Rex with a crown imperial, illumined and finished with a globe of fire.' Inside Loosely's tavern was a transparency of their majesties 'with a crown supported by angels elegantly illuminated by different colored lights', while at the King's Head a band played *God Save the King* every hour.[29]

[27] Van Schaack, *Life*, pp. 238–9, 241–2, 249–50, 258–60, 322.
[28] Prince William's visit furnished an occasion for one of the worst of the generally execrable Tory verses published in Rivington's *Royal Gazette*; a memorable couplet ran as follows:

> Rising o'er the Atlantic main,
> William, the star of Morn, appears.

Quoted in Van Tyne, *Loyalists*, p. 288.   [29] *Ibid.*, pp. 264–5.

There is little question that, despite such effusions of sentiment as these, most of the Loyalist refugees, whether in New York, England, Halifax, or elsewhere, would have been glad to make their peace with the new United States. During the long period of suspenseful unease between the end of fighting and the conclusion of a peace settlement, the Loyalists lost much of what remained of their enthusiasm for their cause. They felt abandoned and betrayed by Britain, as is suggested by this bitter little rhyme of the day:

> 'Tis an honor to serve the bravest of nations,
> And be left to be hanged in their capitulations.[30]

Feeling that they deserved better, the refugees had to depend on the fitful charity of the government, not knowing how long even this would continue. 'We are obliged', wrote Peter Oliver, 'to put up with every insult from this ungrateful people the English without any redress.'[31]

At the same time the Loyalists were astonished and dismayed at the undiminished rancour of their republican countrymen. Some Tories who attempted to return to their former homes were driven away or threatened with mob violence; a few became victims of judicial murder, and in the South a number of others were killed with less formality. Even some passive Loyalists who had remained unmolested through the war years, presumably as their neighbours' insurance against a British victory, were now forced to leave. In Pennsylvania nearly five hundred Tories had been attainted for high treason *in absentia*, while in other states the Tory leaders and many of the rank and file were forbidden to return by Acts of Banishment which, in some cases, remained on the books until after the War of 1812.[32]

It is true that some of the refugees, especially those who had taken no active part in the war, could and did return home.

---

[30] Quoted, Van Tyne, *Loyalists*, p. 288.
[31] Quoted, Einstein, *Divided Loyalties*, p. 235.
[32] Van Tyne, *Loyalists*, pp. 269–95.

Van Schaack was welcomed back to the cosmopolitan society of New York and 'sought after with avidity' for his news of the great world of Burke and Fox, of Mrs. Siddons and Hannah More, and of Sir Joshua Reynolds and Dr. Johnson. He seems to have had no regrets at his return, living on in New York until his death in 1832. Other New York Tories, like Josiah Hoffman, who later became the state's attorney-general, and his law partner, Cadwallader Colden (Governor Colden's grandson), were, as respectable Federalists, to carry on the traditions of an official class until after 1800. Even Samuel Seabury returned once again to New York as a missionary of the Church of England, now become merely Episcopal.[33]

Samuel Curwen, having not been included in the Massachusetts Act of Banishment, was one of comparatively few New England Tories who could return if he wished. He was not entirely happy at the prospects of life, either in England or America. 'I can view neither country without the most fearful apprehensions of dreadful distresses', he wrote. Still, early in 1783 he began to dissociate himself from his fellow refugees, no longer attending their meetings or going to the New England Coffee House. He slipped off to look at the 'American thirteen stripes' flying on some vessels in the Thames, 'the first view I ever distinctly had'. When the Treasury agreed to continue paying him his pension in America, he wrote good-bye to his one English friend, and went back to Salem. There, everything seemed unaccountably 'low, mean, and diminutive' compared with London; alarming social changes had taken place, and Curwen found himself 'completely ruined'. He wrote caustically of the new rulers of Massachusetts that, 'their little minds are not equal to the astonishing success of their feeble arms'. He decided, he wrote to Sewell, to go to Nova Scotia; but instead he lived on in Salem for almost twenty years, irreconcilably miserable.[34]

[33] D. R. Fox, *The Decline of Aristocracy in the Politics of New York* (New York, 1919), pp. 12–14; Van Schaack, *Life*, p. 392; Beardsley, *Life of Seabury*, p. 74.   [34] Curwen, *Journal*, pp. 259, 373, 412–17.

Those Loyalists who could not, or would not, make peace with the United States had to make other arrangements. From habit and necessity, they looked to Britain to provide for them. 'This huge unwieldy Town swarms with Americans grumbling & discontented', wrote one Loyalist of London in 1784. They complained of British slowness and niggardliness in settling their claims: 'The unfortunate people who have come to England and thrown themselves on Government', wrote one Tory to another, 'have been dealt to with a very sparing hand, & others who come at this late hour I am sure will not fare better.'[35] In the end, of course, Britain generously compensated the Loyalists for their losses in America, paying out nearly twenty million dollars in claims. More than money, however, what the Loyalist exiles required was a place in which to settle. Some few were able to fit into the tightly woven society of England, or to find careers in the army or navy. Several thousand Tories, mostly from the Southern states, went to the West Indies. There was even a plan, which Lord Sydney discouraged, for a Loyalist colony in Australia. By far the greater number of refugees, however, settled eventually in what remained of British North America, most of them in Nova Scotia and what became New Brunswick.[36]

Even Jonathan Sewell, once he had some other place to go, quickly lost his passion for England: 'I am tired of England', he wrote, '& earnestly long once more to see you and others of my old American friends & acquaintances, I mean in Nov. Sco. & N. Brun.; for as for those in the 13 States, 2 or 3 excepted, I have not a wish to see a devil of them in this world or the next.' The Tories began with high hopes for the future of their new provinces, writing to each other that 'Nova Scotia will yet be the seat of happiness and the residence of honest Fellows', and that the government of New Brunswick 'shall be

[35] *Winslow Papers*, pp. 166, 174.
[36] Van Tyne, *Loyalists*, pp. 288–9; W. H. Siebert, *The Legacy of the American Revolution to the British West Indies and Bahamas* (Columbus, 1913); H. Davies, 'American Loyalists and Australia', *United Empire*, xxv. 248–50; see also Wright, *The Loyalists of New Brunswick*.

the most Gentlemanlike one on earth'. 'By Heaven', Edward Winslow wrote, 'we will be the envy of the American States.'[37] These brave expectations were not entirely fulfilled, although few Loyalist settlers could afford to admit this final disillusionment. 'I am in the midst of as chearful a society as any in the world', Winslow wrote firmly; 'we are not . . . in the least danger of starving, freezing, or being blown into the Bay of Fundy'.[38] Yet a Loyalist woman wrote, 'I climbed to the top of Chipman's Hill and watched the sails disappear in the distance, and such a feeling of loneliness came over me that though I had not shed a tear through all the war I sat down on the damp moss with my baby on my lap and cried bitterly.'[39]

[37] 'Letters of Jonathan Sewell', pp. 426–7; *Winslow Papers*, pp. 100, 172, 193. See also the writer's article, 'The Last Hopes of the American Loyalists', *Canadian Historical Review*, xxxii. 22–42.

[38] *Winslow Papers*, pp. 357–8.

[39] Quoted, A. G. Bradley, *Colonial Americans in Exile* (New York, 1932), p. 121.

CHAPTER IX

The Tory Legacy

It is no easy thing to compare the point of view of the losers in a civil war with that of the victors. For the losers and the victors not only differ objectively in their accounts of the same events, they differ subjectively in that they remember different events, in different sequence, with different emphasis. Above all, they begin with different presuppositions, and these they seldom mention. They do not, in fact, truly argue with each other; had they done so, they probably would not have fought.

Out of the events of the American Revolution, viewed in a particular light, the revolutionists and their spiritual descendants constructed the foundations of an American national tradition. Their interpretation of the Revolution has been refined and revised by later historians, challenged in many of its particulars, and on occasion circumvented. In its fundamental propositions, however, it has not been displaced, and it remains a classic Whig interpretation of American history.

During and after the Revolutionary War a number of Loyalist writers set forth their own interpretation of the Revolution. They discussed its origins, described its course, as they saw it, and speculated on its implications. The political and intellectual climate of the day was not congenial to their views, so that these never grew, as otherwise they might have done, into a Tory interpretation of American history. They remain an unread testament, containing an uncollected legacy.

The Whig historians of the Revolution contended that America had been forced to assert its independence in order to maintain its political freedom. They cited British policies after 1763, particularly Parliament's attempts to tax the colonies, as

Whig historians use Parliaments attempts to tax the colonies to prove their point that Amer. were forced to seek independence.

primary evidence of a threat to American liberty. The revolutionists thus put the main responsibility for the Revolution on the British government, and regarded American actions as essentially defensive. The Tories, on the other hand, thought America had played an active and aggressive part in bringing on the Revolution, and blamed Britain for having encouraged rebellion by neglect and lax administration.

The Loyalist writers agreed that America, on the eve of the Revolution, was a fortunate country. 'At the time it broke out', Galloway wrote of the Revolution, 'the people in the Colonies were more free, unincumbered and happy than any others on earth.' Hutchinson wrote that Massachusetts was never freer of 'real evils' than in 1772.[1] The Anglican clerics, even while recommending non-resistance to oppression, insisted that in America there had been no oppression.

To be sure, much of the Loyalists' idealization of American life as it was before the Revolution ought to be discounted as the fond recollecting of a comfortable past by men whom events had made uncomfortable. Yet some of the Tory praise of pre-revolutionary America has a certain interest, like this rather romantic encomium of Crèvecœur's:

Here we have in some measure regained the ancient dignity of our species. . . . In this great American asylum the poor of Europe have by some means met together. . . . Formerly they were not numbered in any civil lists of their country, except in those of the poor; here they rank as citizens. . . . Here are no aristocratical families, no courts, no kings, no bishops. . . . We are a people of cultivators, united by the silken bands of mild government, all respecting the laws, without dreading their power, because they are equitable. . . . We are the most perfect society now existing in the world.[2]

It has not always been made clear by the writers who have quoted this passage of Crèvecœur's that he was writing about

[1] Galloway, *Historical Reflections*, pp. 3–4; Hosmer, *Life of Hutchinson*, p. 224.
[2] Crèvecœur, *Letters*, pp. 9, 49–53.

America before the Revolution. The established immigrant, he continued imaginatively, would reflect on his well-being while 'with a heartfelt gratitude he looks toward the east, toward that insular government from whose wisdom all his new felicity is derived'. The Revolution itself Crèvecœur regarded with incomprehension, and the grievances of the revolutionists he described as mythical: 'The whole has been gilded by deception', he wrote, 'and now forms a singular phantom.'[3]

Since they maintained that the Revolution could not appeal 'to antecedent injustice nor oppression for an excuse',[4] the Tories were obliged to find another explanation for it. Here they began by distinguishing sharply, as the revolutionists did not, between negative and positive features of the revolutionary movement. They regarded the Revolution in its negative aspect as an explosion of destructive energies, having no ultimate aim. Underlying this mere rebellion, however, they thought they discovered a positive and coherent plan for the establishment of American independence.

The Tory writers held that rebellion was latent in any society; its outbreak in America they ascribed to the coalescence of two primary forces: first, the weakness of social institutions in America, in particular the weakness of government; and second, the influence of current libertarian ideas imported from Europe. Underlying these was the universal discontent of human nature. In remarking on the universal qualities of the Revolution, the Loyalist writers used quite different terms from those of the revolutionists themselves. Instead of rising out of a natural human love for liberty, rebellions were caused, Boucher wrote, by the readiness of people to be led astray by ambitious, mad, or factious men. 'The politic, like the natural body', Galloway wrote rather pompously, 'is liable to disorders, which often terminate in death.' Hutchinson wrote simply that 'there will be some restless spirits in all governments'.

3 Crèvecœur, *Letters*, pp. 79–80; id., *Sketches*, p. 281.
4 Galloway, *Historical Reflections*, p. 3.

Boucher observed that in its leading features the American Revolution was a clear counterpart of the English Grand Rebellion. He wrote that Lord Clarendon's views were perfectly applicable to the American rebellion, 'as far as the philosophy of history is concerned'. There was also, Boucher thought, a natural likelihood of a colony rebelling against its parent state. He quoted Thucydides on Corcyra's quarrel with Corinth, and concluded that in Corcyra's arguments was the best case that ever could be advanced on behalf of America.[5]

There were, the Loyalists thought, various historical circumstances that had made rebellion easy in America. One was the traditional weakness of British colonial administration. While the revolutionists recalled this as evidence of a lapsed British liberality, the Loyalists regarded it as a delinquency. To them there was nothing salutary in Walpole's vaunted negligence. Galloway, contradicting his own idealization of pre-revolutionary America, complained that the colonists had been allowed to drift into the 'lowest and most imperfect of all political systems, a tumultuous, seditious, and inert democracy'. He wrote that instead of three branches of government, nicely independent of each other, 'the two highest in order, and most dignified, are dependent on the lowest and meanest'. Boucher agreed, writing that the executive branch of government in America had never had any 'Pith and Energy' to it. It was perhaps inevitable, he wrote, that in the early days of the colonies too much weight should have been given to popular institutions, but he thought this should have been corrected as the colonies matured. Instead, successive governments in England had shirked the task of colonial reform, each hoping that nothing would happen until after its time. Eventually, Boucher wrote, the 'latent mischief' had broken out with irresistible force.[6]

[5] Boucher, *Causes*, pp. xxv–xxviii, li; Galloway, *Historical Reflections*, p. 1; Hosmer, *Life of Hutchinson*, p. 120.
[6] Galloway, *Historical Reflections*, pp. 32, 39; 'Letters of Jonathan Boucher', viii. 247; Boucher, *Causes*, p. xxxvii.

Several Tory writers observed that the establishment of parliamentary supremacy in England had led to a deterioration of the government's authority in the colonies. The Maryland Loyalist historian, George Chalmers, wrote that after the Revolution of 1688 the English had been inhibited in their colonial policy by their own distrust of arbitrary government: 'The principles which had been propagated', he wrote, '. . . the insurrections which had been countenanced . . . really enfeebled parliamentary power.'[7] Hutchinson wondered whether the colonies of a country whose constitution had a popular basis would not inevitably be dissatisfied with anything less than autonomy. Such discontent, he thought, would necessarily increase as the colonies grew, and would, in turn, be encouraged by the home government's own scruples in exercising its powers.[8]

Chalmers was the only Loyalist writer to consider in detail the history of British administration in America. He found it a lamentable tale of weakness, and decided that this weakness had been of primary importance in producing conditions favourable to revolution. He realized, he wrote, that oppressive rather than negligent government was popularly supposed to cause rebellions, but this he questioned: 'It is curious', he wrote, 'to trace the cause, why forms, thus liberal in their creation, . . . should have given rise to contest, to refractoriness, and at length to civil war.' Chalmers thought that the reign of William III had been the crucial time in the history of Britain's relations with the American colonies. Before 1688 the political troubles in England had precluded the establishment of an efficient colonial administration; after William's reign the maturation of the colonies themselves inhibited British policy. Chalmers described the government's haphazard attempts at colonial reform in this period, but wrote that the colonial constitutions had scarcely been formed,

[7] George Chalmers, *An Introduction to the History of the Revolt of the American Colonies* (2 vols., Boston, 1845), i. 308–9.

[8] Hosmer, *Life of Hutchinson*, p. 229.

'when they were attacked by encroachment and resigned to their fate by neglect'. The series of British distractions in Europe, beginning with the wars of William, had allowed the colonies to become accustomed to autonomy. Chalmers quoted Governor Hunter of New York as warning in 1711 that 'from being provincial and dependent', the colonies would, if unchecked in their ambitions, become 'national and independent'.

The Board of Trade, Chalmers observed, had tried repeatedly to bring about a general reform of colonial administration, having proposed as early as 1696 the appointment of a 'captain-general' to supervise the colonies and strengthen the authority of the governors. Although this proposal was repeated in 1701, 1721, and 1754, nothing was done, Chalmers wrote, and the Board of Trade itself had been, he thought, 'systematically degraded'. Year after year, he wrote, one ministry after another had ignored the explicit warnings of colonial officials that the colonies were establishing their independence. The Duke of Newcastle, for example, had been told in 1740 'that Massachusetts is a kind of commonwealth, where the king is hardly a stadtholder'; while the governor of New Hampshire had written to the Board of Trade 'that it was necessary to convince the people of the plantations, that a state of independency does not become them'. In 1752 the Board of Trade had reported that in New York the most essential powers of government had been 'transferred' to the Assembly; in New Jersey it was reported that the people were 'by principle adverse to kingly government', and in Pennsylvania that the Assembly was 'intoxicated with power'; 'levelling principles' prevailed in South Carolina; government was weak in North Carolina.

Here was a state of things, Chalmers concluded gloomily, 'of which the annals of the world had shown no example', where the authority of government was constantly evaded and challenged from generation to generation. During the whole time, Chalmers wrote, Parliament had continued to make unreal commercial regulations for the colonies, unaware that without political reform, these were both irritating and ineffectual.

Chalmers decided that by 1763, when Parliament attempted to revive its authority, British administration in America was too weak to withstand any vigorous popular opposition.[9]

The weakness of government in America was, to the loyal Anglican clergy, part of a more general feebleness of social institutions, of which the precarious standing of the Church of England was perhaps the most significant. Where there was no loyalty to the Church, Boucher wrote, there could not be loyalty to the State. He lamented the absence of bishops in the colonies, and the poverty and indifferent discipline of the Church. Americans, he wrote, were 'not sufficiently aware of the importance of externals in religion'; church services were 'narrow and contracted'; buildings, 'ordinary and mean'. In the South the discipline of the Church of England was more nearly Presbyterian than Episcopal, and the ministers had to cater to the tastes of their congregations to an undignified degree: 'Voice and action . . . almost constantly carried it.' With so little attention given to the Church, it was small wonder, Boucher thought, that nothing was 'so wholly without form or comeliness, as government in America'.[10]

Related to the weakness of the Church, Boucher thought, were numerous imperfections in American education. He remarked on the woefully small attention paid to education in Virginia, where there had been no real colleges and few schools, and where most of the schoolmasters had been transported convicts or indentured servants. Having no schools of their own, the Southerners had gone north for their education. The colleges at Philadelphia and Princeton which manufactured physicians and clergymen with equal and indifferent ease, and where 'lawyers seemed to grow up spontaneously', were, Boucher wrote, the 'chief nurseries of all that frivolous and mischievous kind of knowledge which passed for learning in America'. They were 'Seminaries of Sedition', whose chief

[9] Chalmers, *History of the Revolt*, i. 220, 223–6, 271, 413–14; ii. 4, 42–43, 254–7.
[10] Boucher, *Causes*, pp. xliv, 102, 150–1, 232; id., *Reminiscences*, p. 102.

accomplishment had been to corrupt the young Southerners who attended them. The revolutionists in the South, Boucher wrote, had been usually 'young men of Good Parts, but spoil'd by a strange, imperfect, desultory kind of Education'.

Boucher went further than the other Tory writers in regarding the frailty of Church and State as part of a more basic weakness of colonial society itself. America, he wrote, had been settled by people of a multitude of races who, in order to communicate at all, had acquired a dangerously superficial common culture. Americans, he wrote, were 'less attached to each other, and the bond of social or political union is lower there, than in almost any other country'. American society, he concluded, had not acquired a sufficiently tight weave to withstand the individualism of the times.[11]

Here, the Tories thought, was where the liberal notions of the Enlightenment had had a most corrosive influence on colonial society. While they admitted that in the old and settled countries of Europe, the political liberalism of England and the intellectual liberalism of France might have been desirable catalysts, they held that in America these ideas had weakened dangerously the already fragile bonds of social union. Indeed, European liberals were, to the Tories, the unwitting *agents provocateurs* of the Revolution. 'I know not how, with any shew of justice,' Boucher wrote, 'to dissociate the views of the actual revolters in America from those of their abettors in Europe . . . it is not easy to determine whether more was done in America or in Europe to promote its [the Revolution's] success.' There was abroad, he wrote, a 'bold and busy spirit of *innovation*'; and the Revolution occurred when it did because of the 'loose principles of the times'.[12]

'The republicans in America', Galloway wrote, 'had their spies, their friends, and their parties in Britain.' While the American radicals had in mind American independence, their friends in England wished to abolish the 'principles of mixed

[11] Ibid., pp. 99, 101–2; *Causes*, pp. 472–3.
[12] Ibid., pp. vi, xliv–xlv, 214.

Boucher claims that the revolution occurred because the principles of the times were too loose —

monarchy'; on both sides of the Atlantic the radicals had worked to establish their respective societies on 'democratical principles'. Hutchinson thought that, long before the American Revolution, the 'spirit of party' in England had got beyond decent bounds, and had turned English politics into a series of little revolutions. He observed that the constant encouragement the American Whigs had received from their English correspondents had often given 'fresh spirits to the friends of liberty, and perplexed the friends to government'. He thought that the opposition to government in America had developed from the example of English opposition, and once wrote to an English friend, 'When your political frenzy is over, I hope ours will abate.' Another time he wrote simply, in a general explanation of American rebelliousness, 'It is an age of liberty.'[13]

If, however, they thought that the 'loose principles of the times' acting on the weakness of American society had provoked the Revolution, the Tory writers found another explanation for American independence. While the revolutionists regarded independence as a simple and logical consequence of the Revolution, the Tories maintained that the revolutionary movement had merely provided sufficient confusion and disorder for the proponents of independence to carry through their project. Independence itself, they believed, was the result of a 'settled plan', formed by the New England Puritans, to establish an American nation separate from Britain which was to be dominated by New England. The people of the Southern Colonies, they believed, had been led into rebellion by a misguided, though not ignoble, love of liberty, and had then been manœuvred by the New Englanders into accepting a separation from Britain which they had not desired.

The American Revolution, Galloway wrote, had begun, not in 1775 or 1765, but in the sixteenth century, when the Puritans first broke out of the comprehension of the Church of

[13] Galloway, *Historical Reflections*, p. 60; Hosmer, *Life of Hutchinson*, pp. 190–1; Hutchinson, *History*, iii. 233.

England. Being individualists, and consequently democrats, in religious matters, the Puritans inevitably became political democrats as well. For if a congregation had exclusive power to ordain its priests, the people, Galloway wrote, had to be allowed a similar power to appoint their own civil officials. 'This kind of popular independence in ecclesiastical', he wrote, 'was so nearly allied to that in civil polity, it is scarcely possible to conceive that the human mind could hold the one and reject the other.'[14]

Boucher wrote that the spirit of Puritan republicanism, after plunging England into a blood bath of civil war and anarchy, had been checked there by the Restoration, but had 'ever since fascinated the British world under the not less imposing name of Liberty'. The Puritan emigrants had carried this 'turbulent spirit' in its most virulent form to Massachusetts, where it had flourished. The New Englanders, Boucher thought, had remained fanatical 'Independents' at heart, although there were a few honourable exceptions, 'a few useful plants in a field overrun with weeds'.[15]

Perhaps the most mordant of the Tory critics of New England was that apostate New Englander, Thomas Chandler. The original settlers of New England, he wrote, had been inveterate enemies of the English Church and State, and their sentiments had been preserved from generation to generation by the *Pulpit-Incendiaries* for whom New England was famous. Although, Chandler wrote, many New Englanders had acquired liberal sentiments and freed themselves from the bigotry of their ancestors, the majority of the people had not. Their prejudices against English society had remained intense, and their attitude to government had retained a *'peculiar complexion'*.[16]

Some of the Tory writers thought they found confirmation of New England's anti-British outlook in the laws of the New

---

[14] Galloway, *Historical Reflections*, pp. 3, 24–26.
[15] Boucher, *Causes*, pp. xxix, xxxi.
[16] Chandler, *A Friendly Address*, pp. 29, 30.

England colonies. Galloway observed that, although the New Englanders had laws to enable them to persecute dissenters from their own Puritan discipline, they had no laws for punishing traitors to the King. Chalmers wrote that while the Southern Colonies had generally adopted the laws of England, the New Englanders had founded their laws instead on the harsh precepts of the Old Testament. Chalmers, indeed, developed elaborately the theory that New England was separatist from its foundations. He cited an English complaint of 1635 that the 'New English' aimed not so much 'at new discipline as at sovereignty', and wrote that New England had actually established its independence 'by a singular effort of usurpation' during the troubled reign of Charles I. The Restoration had not really extended to New England, and the final establishment of parliamentary supremacy in England had led to a final deterioration of English authority in New England. During this entire period, Chalmers wrote, the New England clergy, ever notable for their ambition and their 'savage vulgarity', had excited their congregations in a love of equality and impatience of social restraint which had become distinct New England traits.[17]

Outside New England at least, the Tories seem to have been in nearly universal agreement in attributing American independence to a New England conspiracy. This view was held, not only by the Tory writers, but by rank-and-file Tories, like the Maryland farmer who said he believed the people of Boston 'wanted a King of their own in America', or the Delaware man who said he 'had as lief be under a tyrannical King as a tyrannical Commonwealth, especially if the d—d Presbyterians had the rule of it'. More often than not, the Tories regarded this New England scheme as a deliberate, conscious plot. Galloway, for example, wrote that early in their history the New Englanders had made a 'fixed resolution' to establish an independent commonwealth of their own. Chandler wrote

[17] Galloway, *Historical Reflections*, p. 37; Chalmers, *History of the Revolt*, i. 55, 58, 63, 67, 88, 106–7.

that the New Englanders had, for many years, spoken 'in un-
guarded moments' of establishing a republic.[18]

There were, it is true, a few Tory dissenters from the theory
of a New England plot. Hutchinson, for example, wrote that
he did not believe his countrymen had 'laid a regular plan' to
achieve independence, but that he thought only that they had
a general inclination 'as soon as they have carried one point
to attempt another'. And William Smith of New York, while
accepting New England separatism as a fact, pointed out that,
after all, the British had encouraged the settlement of America
by 'civil and religious Enthusiasts', had granted virtually
republican constitutions to the New England colonies and to
Pennsylvania, and had then neglected the colonies until they
had become rich. It was hardly surprising, he wrote, that
Britain's sudden and careless attempts at colonial reform after
1763 should have aroused opposition in what had for a long
time been the independent republics of America.[19]

Taken at its face value, the Tory belief that American independence grew out of an historical conspiracy among New
Englanders is as absurd as the contemporary notion among
the revolutionists that the British government was engaged
in a deliberate plot against American liberty. Just as Lord
North had no intention of subjecting Americans to British
tyranny, so most of the revolutionists, whether New Englanders or not, obviously abhorred the idea of separation from
Britain until, as they thought, British ill-will forced them to
change their minds. Considered in another way, however,
there may be a grain of sense in these conspiratorial theories.
The eighteenth century had no way to express a concept of
historical determinism, except in moral terms. An event which
seemed clearly to fall into a teleological pattern of development was, in the thought of the times, the effect either of
a plan of divine Providence, or of a devilish plot, depending

---

[18] 4 *Am. Arch.* iii. 1072, 1573; Galloway, *Historical Reflections*, pp. 37–38;
Chandler, *What Think Ye?*, pp. 36–37.
[19] Hutchinson, *Diary*, i. 115–16; Smith, *Historical Memoirs*, pp. 247–51.

upon whether it seemed good or bad. If the element of moral praise or reproach is removed, there is, after all, no great difference between the Tory belief that New England Puritanism was in permanent and wicked conspiracy against the British government, and John Adams's belief that the settlement of New England by the Puritans was part of a divine plan for the liberation of man from the tyranny of Church and State. At least both theories agreed that America's relations with Britain were made necessarily uneasy by the acceptance in New England of social values and a political outlook which had been rejected in England.

It is illuminating, in order to see the essential argument of the Revolution, to consider Whig and Tory accounts at their points of greatest divergence: in the views of the Anglican High Tories on the one hand, and in those of the theoreticians of the Revolution on the other. These two groups of writers differ irreconcilably in fundamental premises. They differ not only about the Revolution itself, and revolutions in general: even more deeply, they differ about the essential functions of government, about the proper role of the State, and about the nature of society itself.

The revolutionists thought that individual judgement was competent to challenge and alter corporate authority whenever it seemed necessary to do so. And with varying degrees of confidence and enthusiasm they regarded individual freedom from the tyranny of Church and State as the most compelling of political ends. The High Tories took a quite different view: they lacked faith in the competence of individual judgement, whether founded on reason or feeling, to put the world in better order. They denied that the kind of individual freedom the revolutionists described was possible, for they believed that, in any society, men would be ruled over by an authority, the limits of which could not be set by individual judgement, and over which men, as individuals, could have little control. They thought they had to choose, not between submission to, and freedom from, the claims of corporate authority; but between submission to a traditional authority, restrained by habit and custom, and submission to a new authority, unchecked by law and perhaps supported by violence.

In the writings of John Locke the revolutionists had, of course, found a most persuasive justification of the right of revolution. To the American Whigs, Locke's utilitarian concept of society, combined with his contractual theory of government, and no theory of the State at all, seemed simple common sense. While they accepted his major argument, the revolutionists rejected, however, what Locke had thought he proved: the sovereignty of Parliament. For Locke, the Revolution of 1688 had completed the English Whig epic, and nothing remained for true Whigs to do but bask in the sun of English liberty and enjoy the blessings of mixed government. For the American Whigs, however, the glorious events of 1688 were only a fanfare at the beginning of an American epic. As early as 1765 John Adams, for example, developed a Whig theory of individualism into a creed of American destiny.

Adams thought that the grand theme of European history had been the struggle between individual freedom and corporate authority. The tyranny of corporate authority, he wrote, had been established in the darkness of the Middle Ages by the development of the canon and feudal law. These instruments of 'ecclesiastical and civil tyranny' had conspired with each other to hold people bound in superstition and ignorance. Their confederacy had been mercifully broken when God had raised up the champions of the Reformation. Protestantism had destroyed the corporate authority of the Church, and this in turn had weakened the authority of the State, whose destruction, heralded by the Revolution of 1688, was to be finally and fully achieved in America.

'I always consider the settlement of America with reverence and wonder', Adams wrote, 'as the opening of a grand scene and design in Providence for the illumination of the ignorant, and the emancipation of the slavish part of mankind all over the earth.' He observed that his New England countrymen had already not only demolished the whole system of ecclesiastical tyranny based on the 'ridiculous fancies' of episcopal ordination, but had also organized their governments in disdain of the feudal law. They had had from the first, he wrote, an utter contempt for all 'dark ribaldry about the divine origin of government', and had always known that government was a 'plain, simple, intelligible thing, founded in nature and reason, and quite comprehensible by common sense'. In opposing the British Parliament, therefore, his countrymen, Adams thought, were simply fulfilling their mission as the heirs of all the heroes and martyrs who had fought in the name of individual freedom.[20]

The assumption that America was manifestly destined to fulfil the claims of individual liberty found its most extreme expression in Tom Paine's *Common Sense*. Reasoning, as Locke had done, from the presupposition that man in a state of nature was free, rational, and individual, Paine supposed that society was a voluntary union of convenience, and that government was at best a necessary evil. 'Society', he wrote, 'is produced by our wants, and government by our wickedness . . . Government . . . like dress, is the badge of lost innocence; the palaces of Kings are built on the ruins of the bowers of Paradise.' Since he believed that all social institutions were artificial restraints on individual freedom, Paine regarded the weakness of these institutions in America as highly fortunate. America, he thought, had the chance to become entirely free. For the British emigrants to the colonies had returned to a state of nature the moment they left England, and if they had continued for a while to act like Englishmen, this had been due only to ignorant habit.[21]

The conservative revolutionists did not, of course, entirely approve of Paine. But if they thought some of his assertions extravagant, and criticized his arguments for democracy, they did not reject his individualist theories about society and

[20] Adams, 'Dissertation on the Canon and the Feudal Law', *Works*, iii. 447-64.   [21] Thomas Paine, *Common Sense* (Philadelphia, 1776), *passim*.

government, let alone his assumptions of American destiny. The Tory writers, for their part, could have refuted Paine's arguments for independence without challenging his philosophy. The depth of the extreme Tories' disagreement with the Revolution is suggested by the fact that, in disputing Paine, they went on to dispute Locke, and quarrel generally with the individualism of the times. Charles Inglis, for example, in his reply to *Common Sense*, began by denying that man in a state of nature was free at all. All men, he wrote, were born into society, were under social obligations from the moment of birth, and therefore were not and could not be 'free' in Paine's sense. While Paine had described society as a product of man's wants, Inglis maintained it was a product of his nature: it was the essential state of man. He compared Paine, oddly but shrewdly, with Hobbes, who also believed that natural man was a lone creature, though not, as Paine thought, a happy one. For his part, Inglis rejected Paine, Hobbes, and Locke, in order to agree with Hooker that man's life in society was as divinely constituted as his individual life. Since society could not exist without law, nor law without government, Inglis wrote that government was not a necessary evil, but a necessary good. If government was, as Paine thought, a 'badge of lost innocence', Inglis observed that all the arts of civilization were badges of a lost innocence that must have been, had it ever existed, a state of dreadful savagery.

Having rejected Paine's individualist description of society, Inglis felt himself bound to believe that the Englishmen who had settled the American colonies had been in a continuous state of society, before, during, and after their emigration. They had remained part of English society. 'The Americans', he wrote, 'are properly Britons.' Of Paine's criticism of the English constitution, Inglis, following Montesquieu, asked who had a better constitution for Englishmen, with English laws and habits.[22]

[22] Charles Inglis, *The True Interest of America Impartially Stated* (Philadelphia, 1776), *passim.*

It is significant that Inglis, like most of the Anglican clergy in the Northern Colonies, was a missionary of the Society for the Propagation of the Gospel. The Loyalism of these men has often been dismissed as the prudent, or at best conscientious, performance of their duty by men who were a species of royal official. But there was more to it than that. The Church of England, feeble as it was, and sorely compromised in a secular age by its dependence on secular authority, had managed to keep alive, in its more vital branches, a concept of society different from that of the eighteenth century at large. In the shelter of the Church it was possible to escape the shadow of Locke, possible even to catch occasionally a glimpse of the lost catholic world of Hooker. In opposition to the rationalism and individualism of the age, the Anglicans in America set forth, with true missionary zeal, the idea that society was more than a collection of individual men, and government more than mere useful machinery.

While Inglis argued with Paine, his fellow missionary, Jonathan Boucher, disputed Locke himself. He went about this by patiently exhuming Sir Robert Filmer, whom Locke had been at pains to bury for all time.[23] 'I have lately perused the book', he wrote of *Patriarcha*, 'and did not find it deserving of all that extreme contempt with which it is now the fashion to mention it.' Boucher was impressed with Filmer's arguments for the origin of government in the family, and for the paternal character of all authority. He thought that, despite his 'very extravagant notions on monarchy', Filmer's essential thesis, that men are born not free, but subjects, had not been answered by Locke.

Boucher wrote that Locke and all others who believed that government originated in an agreement of the people, had to face the historical fact that the earliest evidence of any society always showed it dominated by an authoritarian, familial government. He cited in support of this the paternalism of a number of primitive peoples: the early Greeks, the people of

[23] Sir Robert Filmer, *Patriarcha: Or the Natural Power of Kings.*

Sierra Leone, and the American Indians he himself knew who called their chiefs 'father'. He decided that Filmer's theory, which found the origins of government in the 'natural and obvious' precedent of the family, and which had been held by most political thinkers from the time of Aristotle to the end of the Middle Ages, was more convincing than Locke's theory of the social compact. In addition, he discovered, he thought, an inherent contradiction in Locke's theory of consent: the incompatibility of the individual's right of resistance, with his duty of submitting to the rule of the majority. The logical end, Boucher wrote, of Locke's views was a state of anarchy. Therefore, he rejected Locke's 'subtle and uncertain deductions' about the nature of society, and thus necessarily rejected his justification of revolution.[24]

It was not, of course, merely from reading Filmer that Boucher came to believe Locke was wrong. Through his religion he had already, like Inglis, rediscovered medieval social theory, and seen a vision of a world where society was blessed, and man could be saved, not by seeking his own fulfilment only, but by living in grace with his fellows. The revolutionists, on the other hand, like the European individualists whose ideas they shared, had little interest in society as such. It was the life of the individual that was sacred to them, and their theories about society were usually mere projections of their concern for the individual. Conceiving of society almost as a machine, they were eager to learn its secrets, to dismantle it if necessary and rebuild it on rational principles.

The High Tories, for their part, regarded society almost as an organism, a living, breathing thing, its mysteries beyond the wit of man. 'Caution and reverence', Boucher wrote, rather than rational confidence, were necessary in speculating about such matters, for ultimately man had to 'live by faith and not by sight'. While the revolutionists were seeking out and claiming rights for man as an individual, so as to surround him with a sacred circle of defences against corporate authority, the

[24] Boucher, *Causes*, pp. lvii, 518–19, 525–31.

Tories were concerned to point out his duties, and the restraints that ought to be laid upon him to prevent him doing harm to society. Lacking confidence both in individual men and in individual generations of men, they were suspicious of anything that broke through the crust of custom and took people out of their usual habits. They even distrusted large assemblies of men: Jonathan Sewell observed that 'The larger bodies of men are, the more false importance they reflect on each other.' Boucher wrote emphatically that 'Mankind have seldom been assembled in great numbers for any useful purpose.'[25]

To the revolutionists, liberty was a concern of utmost importance, and liberty was to be found in the assertion of the rights of the individual against the priests and princes who would oppress him. The Tories were not indifferent to liberty, but they defined it differently. They believed that men were in more danger of being enslaved by their own unreason than by Church or State. The people themselves, Crèvecœur wrote, might in the hour of infatuation', become the artificers of their own chains. The primary aim of all 'well-framed Constitutions', Boucher wrote, was to place man out of reach of his own power and folly, and also out of the power of men as weak as himself, by putting him under the power of law. Only thus could he enjoy liberty at all, true liberty being a 'severe and a restrained thing', the liberty, as Montesquieu had written, of living under the laws. To attack the authority of government in the name of liberty, Boucher wrote, was absurd: it was to attack liberty itself.[26]

The Tories were impatient of the revolutionists' idealization of man in a state of nature. They saw little that was noble in man, except his civilized attainments, and these they regarded as social products, maintained by the institutions of society, of which government was one. When Boucher wrote that he did not believe the end of government was 'the com-

[25] Boucher, *Causes*, p. 389; id., *Reminiscences*, p. 47; Galloway Papers, Library of Congress, 'Plan, *ca.* 1784', p. 10.
[26] Crèvecœur, *Sketches*, p. 253; Boucher, *Causes*, pp. 363, 509–11.

mon good of mankind', but rather 'the advancement of God's honour', he meant partly that the government ought to sanctify the laws, the traditions, the ceremonies, and usages that distinguished civilized, social man from man in a state of savagery. To the Tories, a 'state of nature' was a condition of darkness where, as Daniel Leonard wrote, man had to conceal himself from his fellow men, inhabit his own cave, and seek his own prey.[27]

It is easy, at a cool distance from the fires of revolution, to see the weaknesses both of the Tory and revolutionist theoreticians. The revolutionists had a very imperfect sense of the strength of existing social arrangements. Society could not be remade in an hour, even if this were desirable; and such social changes as could occur, could not be accurately controlled or predicted. The Tories, on the other hand, by sanctifying all existing social arrangements, made no allowance for the decadence and incapacity of the institutions they revered. Both Paine and Boucher, for example, had romantic and inflated views of monarchy: Paine because he believed that by dismissing kings as 'crowned ruffians', he could safely ignore the whole psychology of state authority; Boucher because he thought it possible to endow George III with the attributes and prerogatives of a sixteenth-century monarch.

It is also obvious that, between the extreme, logical, and perhaps foolish conviction of, say, Boucher on one side, and Paine on the other, were men of all conceivable subtleties of outlook. There were Loyalists like Van Schaack who revered Locke, and revolutionists like Dickinson who revered the King. And there were men on both sides too wise to define the present, or confine the future within their own theories. For out of all the turmoil of revolution and war there did finally emerge an American polity not so very different from what had been known before, and yet not what had been expected by either Whig or Tory.

If there were any serious consequences to America from the silencing and expulsion of the Loyalists, they were certainly

[27] Adams and Leonard, *Novanglus*, p. 188.

not social or, in the narrow sense, political consequences. Rather they were philosophical consequences: the Tories' organic conservatism represented a current of thought that failed to reappear in America after the Revolution. A substantial part of the whole spectrum of European social and political philosophy seemed to slip outside the American perspective. But it would be a mistake to attribute the absence of a conservative tradition in America to the suppression of the Tories. For their exclusion was not so much a cause as a confirmation and an illustration of an alarming uniformity of outlook in America. In any case, there was a certain impoverishment in the failure of American society to include, to comprehend, the Tories.

Index